Vienna

320 m / 0.2 miles

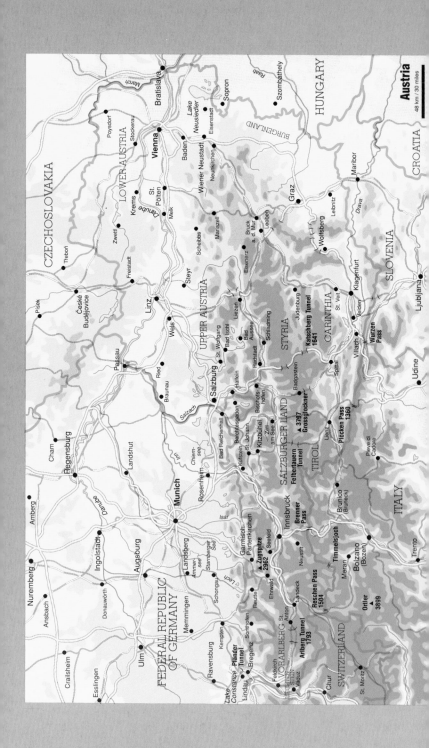

Austria

48 km / 30 miles

INSIGHT *pocket* GUIDES

Vienna

Written and Presented by **Nicole Schmidt**

INSIGHT
pocket
GUIDES

Insight Pocket Guide:

VIENNA

Directed by
Hans Höfer

Managing Editor
Andrew Eames

Photography by
Nicole Schmidt and others

Design Concept by
V Barl

© 1993 APA Publications (HK) Ltd

All Rights Reserved

Printed in Singapore by
Höfer Press (Pte) Ltd
Fax: 65-8616438

Distributed in the United States by
Houghton Mifflin Company
2 Park Street
Boston, Massachusetts 02108
ISBN: 0-395-66911-1

Distributed in Canada by
Thomas Allen & Son
390 Steelcase Road East
Markham, Ontario L3R 1G2
ISBN: 0-395-66911-1

Distributed in the UK & Ireland by
GeoCenter International UK Ltd
The Viables Center, Harrow Way
Basingstoke, Hampshire RG22 4BJ
ISBN: 9-62421-556-1

Worldwide distribution enquiries:
Höfer Communications Pte Ltd
38 Joo Koon Road
Singapore 2262
ISBN: 9-62421-556-1

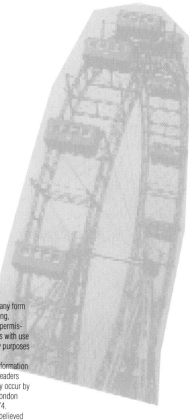

SERVUS!

Welcome! Vienna has always fascinated anyone keen on traditions, magnificent old buildings and romantic city streets. But as a young *Wienerin* (Viennese woman) of 14, I thought the city was like a stuffy museum. Vienna was a sleepy place, its beauties passive and static, and its blinds rolling down with a bang at around 10pm every night.

Now things have changed – and not just my age and tastes. Towards the end of the 1970s the sleeping beauty suddenly woke up. The baroque palaces, the magnificent parks, the narrow, peaceful streets, the art treasures and the largely intact old town are all still there (despite the fire at the end of 1992), but everything is suddenly more lively. With 5,000 or so different bars, pubs and restaurants – ranging from smoke-filled cabaret vaults to chic wine bars, and from gourmet temples to the Old Viennese-style *Beisl* (taverns) – the city has something to suit every taste and mood. My aim in these pages is to give you some idea of the tension between the nostalgia of the city's past and its thrilling present. To this end, I have devised a series of three full day itineraries covering the essential sights, followed by a choice of 12 options. These include visits to Schönbrunn and Belvedere, to Vienna's markets and several of its famous *Jugendstil* (art nouveau) buildings, its museums and coffee houses. The Practical Information section at the back contains everything you need to know.

Insight Pocket Guide: Vienna is not designed to regiment your stay, but to act as a catalyst. You can stick closely to its suggestions, but I hope it will stimulate you into making discoveries of your own.

Servus! Welcome! — Nicole Schmidt

Contents

Preceding pages:
St Stephen's Cathedral in winter   **6**

Following pages:
society ball

Romans and Habsburgs

Vienna has its strategic location on the banks of the Danube to thank for its 2,000-year history. In 15BC the Romans pitched the military camp of Vindobona on the site of today's District 1. When Leopold I of Babenberg, Heinrich Jasomirgott, transferred his seat there in 1155, Vienna quickly developed into a prosperous town. It stood at the crossroads of the trading routes between East and West, between the Levant, Italy and the North, and in the 14th century it became the seat of the Habsburg dynasty. In 1365 Rudolf IV, the 'Founder', endowed the second university in the German-speaking world, now known as the 'Alte Universität', in Vienna.

In the year 1529 the Ottoman army attempted to take the city. Thanks to an early winter, it was successfully repulsed. After this, new fortifications were erected. Remains of these city bastions, which were built in the Renaissance style, are still in existence to-day (eg the Mölkerbastei). In the middle of the 16th century Kaiser Ferdinand established the Jesuits in Vienna. In the fight against Protestantism they soon had the city's cultural and educational life firmly under control: Vienna developed into a stronghold of Catholicism. The so-called 'fortress of the Occident' succeeded in standing up to an attack by the Ottoman army for a second time in 1683. The rubble and ash the Turks left behind in the suburbs now became the foundations of magnificent palaces that were erected for the nobility by Baroque master builders such as Lukas von Hildebrandt and Johann Bernhard Fischer von Erlach. The Upper and Lower Belvederes and the palace of Schönbrunn were built at this time. Craftsmen streamed into Vienna from all over the empire – and stayed there.

The city's flourishing artistic and cultural life reached its high point at the beginning of the 18th century. Under Maria Theresa, Vienna developed its own power base. Her son Joseph II restrained the power of the Jesuits in favour of the Enlightenment. At the be-

Culture

ginning of the 19th century, Napoleon occupied the city; his final defeat was sealed at the famous Congress of Vienna in 1815.

The Biedermeier Period

The first half of the 19th century is today known as the Biedermeier Period. State Chancellor Metternich, with his secret police, presided over everything from the Ballhausplatz, and 'der gute Kaiser Franz', who considered any form of new idea inherently suspect, was entrenched in the Hofburg. Perhaps no epoch in retrospect has been so cliché-ridden as the period between the festive Congress of Vienna and the burning barricades of 1848, the year of revolutions throughout Europe.

The comfortable middle classes were not as naive as all that, though: they could see that within the straitjacket of the police state and reactionary state power there was a two-faced attitude to life. After all, just as much a part of this comfortable Biedermeier period were Beethoven's rebellious genius, Ferdinand Raimund's

Historical Vienna

The Meat Market

amusing magic theatre and Peter Fendi's 'pornographic' drawings. The prevailing mood was a tension between extreme subservience on the one hand, and on the other, the satirical rebelliousness of, say, Johann Nestroy. And while all this was going on, the age of the steam engine and of proletarian misery was gradually dawning.

In March 1848, bloody revolution broke out in the city. Townspeople, workers and students all rose up against repression. Metternich and the royal family fled; they retaliated, however, as early as October. By the end of 1848, the 18-year-old Franz Joseph's accession to the throne was proclaimed. The beginning of his reign was marked by a period of neo-absolutism.

In 1857 Franz Joseph had the old defensive walls torn down – the city was gradually expanding. The walls were replaced by Vienna's magnificent boulevard, the Ringstrasse. The *Gründerzeit* epoch or Vienna's great expansion was at its height. Architects and builders were streaming into Vienna from all over Europe and turning the city into a melting-pot once again. Building styles also blended into each other. Historicism was all the rage: the Opera House and the new Burgtheater were built in a mixture of neo-classical and Italian Renaissance styles, the Town Hall was given Neo-Gothic towers, and the Parlament (parliament building) was built in the Greek Revival style.

The exciting atmosphere of the *Gründerzeit* also affected municipal policy. In 1860 Vienna had its first ever Liberal mayor, and Otto Wagner's *Jugendstil* (the Viennese version of *art nouveau*) buildings, such as the Secession Building and the Postsparkasse (Post Office Savings Bank), set entirely new architectural accents.

This boom in investment had its darker side, however: the working class lived in misery, in sub-standard housing. A cholera epidemic and a stock exchange crash put an end to the economic boom as well as the Vienna World Fair. The recession was a home-made one, at least in part. Technologically, Vienna was limping along behind most other cities. Its *petit bourgeoisie* was concentrating on the struggle against industry and finance, and took refuge in anti-semitic feeling. Very soon all the pomp and finery became riddled with corruption, while at the same time art and philosophy flourished as never before under such figures such as Gustav Klimt and Otto Wagner, Adolf Loos and Josef Hoffmann, Sigmund Freud and Arthur Schnitzler. Vienna's Jewish community provided the city with that famous *fin de siècle* culture that the world still talks about today.

Racism and Fascism

In 1895 Karl Lueger ('I decide who's Jewish and who isn't'), representing the anti-capitalist *petit bourgeoisie*, was voted mayor of Vienna. The Austro-Hungarian Empire was teetering on the brink of collapse, and its various subject peoples were seething with discontent. The assassination of the successor to the throne, Franz Ferdinand, was a welcome excuse – rather than the real reason – for World War I. In 1916 Emperor Franz Joseph died after 68 years in power. His grand-nephew Karl was forced to leave the country at the end of the war and the Austro-Hungarian Empire came apart at the seams. Suddenly, Vienna was nothing more than the self-important and overblown centre of a giant administrative system that had ceased to exist.

Universal suffrage, introduced in 1919, gave the Social Democrats the majority in the Gemeindeparlament (City Parliament). 'Red Vienna', as it was now called, set up kindergartens and exemplary housing projects such as the Karl-Marx-Hof, which is still considered a milestone in public-assistance housing even today. Alongside all this, however, the seed of Fascism was steadily growing. Seemingly irreconcilable differences between the Christian Socialists and the Social Democrats led to shooting in the streets and finally, in 1934, to civil war. The Austro-Fascist regime under Engelbert Dollfuss took over.

In 1938 Hitler marched into Vienna. Thousands had to flee for their lives; many were deported and murdered. Before World War II there were 170,000 Jews in Vienna; today there are only around 6,000 still living in the city. In April 1945 the Red Army liberated Vienna and the Allies divided up the city into four zones of occupation. One fifth of Vienna's houses had been destroyed, and the Opera House and the roof of St Stephen's Cathedral were in flames.

Several of the former rival politicians from the Social Democratic Party (now called the SPÖ) and the Christian Socialist Party (now the ÖVP) had spent time with one another in concentration camps, and being in the same boat had made them decide to forget their old differences. With patience and diplomatic skill, Austria won back its independence. On 15 May 1955 Federal

Rooftiles of St Stephen's Cathedral

Historical Highlights

5000BC First traces of human settlement.

15BC The Emperor Augustus conquers the kingdom of Noricum, the area of present-day Vienna.

AD100 The Romans set up the military garrison of Vindobona as defence against the Germanic tribes; a town grows up around it.

5th century The Huns conquer Vienna; the Roman Empire collapses, Roman troops leave Vindobona.

881 First mention of Vienna.

10th century Emperor Otto I names the region a frontier area of his kingdom against the East.

1137 Vienna is granted municipal status.

1155 Vienna becomes the seat of the Babenberg dynasty.

1282 Habsburg rule begins.

1359 Rudolf IV, the 'Founder', lays the foundation stone for the Gothic nave of St Stephen's Cathedral.

1365 Vienna University – the second university in the German-speaking world – is founded.

1438 Vienna becomes a residency.

1529 First Turkish siege; the city is refortified in following decades.

Mid-16th century The Reformation also reaches Vienna.

1577 Jesuits 'recatholicise' Vienna.

1679 Plague causes havoc.

1683 Second Turkish siege.

1740 Maria Theresa becomes Empress.

1766 The Prater is opened to the general public.

1805/9 Napoleonic occupation.

1814–15 Congress of Vienna.

1848 A popular uprising overthrows Metternich; Emperor Franz Joseph takes the throne.

1857 The city's old defensive walls are knocked down; construction work begins on the Ringstrasse.

1865 Festive opening ceremony for a section of the Ringstrasse.

1873 The World Fair is a failure due to the stock exchange crash and a cholera epidemic.

1896 The giant Ferris Wheel is installed in the Prater.

1914 Murder of Franz Ferdinand in Sarajevo provides the excuse for World War I.

1916 Emperor Franz Joseph dies, his grand-nephew Karl takes over.

1918 The Austro-Hungarian monarchy collapses; the Emperor leaves Austria; on 12 November the first republic is declared.

1919 Universal suffrage introduced; the Social Democrats rule Vienna until 1934 (civil war).

1922 Vienna becomes an independent federal state in its own right.

1934 Civil war between Social Democrats and Christian Socialists.

1938 Hitler annexes Austria on 14 March *(Anschluss)*.

1945 The Red Army liberates Vienna; the city is divided into four zones of occupation.

15 May 1955 State Treaty *(Staatsvertrag)*.

26 October 1955 Permanent neutrality approved by Austrian constitutional law (a national holiday).

1961 Kennedy/Krushchev summit.

1969 Construction work begins on the city's U-Bahn system.

1979 UN-City opened. Vienna becomes the third most important UN centre. Brezhnev/Carter summit.

1986–9 4th KSZE (European Security and Cooperation Conference).

May 1991 The Viennese reject the idea of hosting Expo 1995.

August 1991 Austria starts negotiations to join the EC.

1992 Fire destroys much of the Hofburg; repairs are swift.

Chancellor Figl waved the signed State Treaty *(Staatsvertrag)* from the balcony of the Belvedere. Reconstruction could now continue with renewed vigour. But the threat posed by the proximity of the Iron Curtain was ever-present. People took refuge in a form of apathy, and the whole country fell into a kind of post-imperial torpor. Renewed self-confidence was slow in coming; even after the initial euphoria at the collapse of the Iron Curtain had subsided it seemed for a while as if the old anxiety was returning. In 1990 there were sudden calls for compulsory visas and drastic cuts in immigration.

Vienna has spent a long time indulging in its undisputed function as a bridgehead for contact with the East; now that the term 'Central Europe' is becoming widely accepted it is going to have to redefine its position and 'compete' anew with Prague and Budapest, its former rivals during Empire days. It is a challenge for the next millennium, and one that can only do the city good.

The Viennese Character

One disadvantage of clichés is that they deprive you of your free, unprejudiced view of things, and automatically affect each one of your later impressions; an advantage they do have, though, is that they can act as a sort of guide through forests of false appearances. And, clichés or no clichés, Vienna certainly does have its share of false appearances.

The Viennese character is a mixture of noisy self-confidence and inferiority complexes – the gratified *Mir san mir* ('we are who we are') attitude, that sense of having once been the centre of the world, mingled with the shock of having suddenly been pushed onto the sidelines of Europe. Now those sidelines have disappeared and the Iron Curtain has vanished, but that itself has created a whole new set of problems, because change quite often tends to bring competition along in its wake. Suddenly Prague and Budapest, the city's former rival, which it had successfully upstaged for so long, are back in the running. And fair competition has never been one of Vienna's strong points.

The Viennese prefer to daydream about change than to welcome it once it's actually happened. 'Things have always been that way.' They grumble about the status quo, but there again, they've adapted to it very nicely. Change is considered troublesome and only ever really gets acknowledged once it's already over and done with. Until the new becomes properly old, makeshift solu-

Waluliso, one of Vienna's eccentrics

tions apply. Things can always be better assimilated in retrospect: Beethoven has become an Austrian, Hitler a German, and the enormous cheering crowd welcoming the Nazi leader on the Heldenplatz in 1938 is forgotten. Conflicts have remained unresolved.

Hardly any city in the world has contributed more to 20th-century thought than Vienna, and hardly any city has shown itself less appreciative of its creative and intellectual elite. People like Otto Wagner and Adolf Loos, Klimt and Schiele, Werfel, Musil, Freud and Schönberg, Wittgenstein, Karl Kraus and Josef Hoffmann; Vienna likes to boast of these names today. Unfortunately, such great Viennese thinkers have had to be acknowledged outside their country first before gaining acceptance there, and their current popularity is only retrospective. Helmut Qualtinger's legendary sentence sums it up: 'In Wien mußt erst sterben, damit's dich hochleben lassen, aber dann lebst lang'. ('In Vienna you need to die before you become popular, but once you're dead you live a long time.')

As time goes by this rejection of anything new gradually turns into parochial approval. Buildings that were once the object of passionate dispute, such as the Opera House or the Loos House, are now old enough to be shown off proudly, but contemporary Viennese architects like Hans Hollein, Gustav Peichl or Wilhelm Holzbauer have to do most of their work abroad. Until recently the sum total of Hollein's work in Vienna was a few shop-fronts. His Haas-Haus on the Stephansplatz was only given building permission once the mayor had given his approval – beer-hall critics regarded anything modern at all in the heart of the city as blasphemy. In 100 years' time, though, the Viennese will probably be as proud of their Hollein as they are of their Opera House today.

Having to make continual compromises can often be intellectually rewarding, but it's when one's patience is finally at an end that the leap to greatness is often achieved and a brilliant mind steps out of the shadows that it seemed to need in order to shine. That's Viennese dialectics for you. It is no coincidence that Vienna was the place where Musil produced his novel *The Man Without Qualities*, and Freud developed psychoanalysis.

The essence of Vienna is contradiction; fantasy and reality aren't real opposites here at all. In the opinion of late author György Sebestyén: 'Since there's apparently no distinction between reality

16

and game-playing, it's better to treat reality as a game than vice-versa. And when reality becomes just as senseless as its "game version", then the game at least has to be cheerful: after all, it costs the same, and we're all going to die anyway.'

'*Verkauft's mei G'wand, i fahr in Himmel*' ('I'm off to Heaven – sell my clothes') says the fatalistic Viennese, and retreats to the inner sanctuary of his soul along with his deep fried chicken and his wine – for after all, '*Es wird a Wein sein, und wir wer'n nimmer sein*' ('We're all going to die, so let's have another wine').

The Viennese are inveterate grumblers. It's a form of rebellion against 'them up there', cultivated over centuries of being dominated by the imperial court. They mock, certainly, but in the end they always pull themselves together and bow to authority: *Meine Verehrung* (reverence), *Herr Hofrat* (*Hofrat* is the rough equivalent of a Privy Councillor).

The imperial court has long since disappeared, but its heritage has remained to this day: titles are all-important. The genuine *Hofrat* proudly wears his title as the shining badge of his rather tedious civil servant's profession; any *Hofrat* who isn't a genuine one is thought of far less highly. Ordinary teachers in Vienna are referred to as *Professor*, which is why university professors always stick a *univ.* in front of their title. Their respective wives are addressed, even in grocery shops, as *Frau Professor* or *Frau Medizinalrat* regardless of whether or not they may happen to possess a title of their own. In business life one has to be a *Kommerzialrat* at least; the best way to inspire respect is loftily to refer to oneself as *k.u.k. Hoflieferant* (roughly: 'purveyor to the Royal Court') and sport the Habsburg double-headed eagle on one's letterhead.

But even nostalgia for the double-headed eagle is not without its share of complications, especially when it comes to the Austrians' former compatriots from the East. They're quite happy to have tourists visit their country, but would rather have as little as possible to do with *Ausländer* (foreigners). True, the typical inhabitant of Vienna is a superb Central European mixture of a Bohemian grandmother, a Polish aunt and a Levantine merchant – and proud of it. That's something quite different though. He's Viennese, you see…

Das Boot ist voll ('The boat is full') were the rather ugly words that slipped out of the SPÖ general secretary's mouth while he was referring to the rise in immigration from the East. The gentleman in question's surname is Marizzi, and his colleague's name is Cap. The whole government, with names such as Vranitsky and Lacina, Dohnal and Busek, is in itself proof enough of how the Viennese became Viennese in the first place.

The Viennese are also contradictory in their rejection of foreigners. They complain about *die Ausländer* – and the fewer foreigners they know, the louder they'll complain – but at the same time they'll leap to the defence of their Polish cleaning ladies. They'll look down condescendingly on *die Fremden* (strangers) and simultaneously fight to keep a kebab shop on their street corner in business. But beneath the distrust, the melancholy and the grumbling you'll also find a sharp wit, and a talent for improvisation and adaptation which – sometimes at least – has its good side as well. Some people reckon that it was this ability to walk the wobbly tightrope of diplomacy plus all the wine, charm and Viennese *schmäh* that gave the country its freedom in 1955.

All right, it did take over 20 years for the intelligentsia to finally rebel and overcome the *petit bourgeois* fustiness of the post-war era, and create a new cultural and gastronomic scene – but now we're the envy of a lot of other cities as a result. The provincial attitudes one encounters in some parts of the city are still a major obstacle, but so is the all-too-easy escape into the faceless anonymity of a large metropolis.

'Now don't get all matter-of-fact – you can remain personal', as Anton Kuh once put it. If you're good at it, Vienna is the perfect venue for noisy, self-confident show-offs. Anyone without any egocentric ambitions who feels threatened by the meaninglessness of it all can always retreat into their inner sanctuaries and console themselves with Georg Hauptfeld's phrase: 'An intentional lie often comes closer to the truth than the truth itself, which is always doubtful.' *Wien ist anders* (Vienna is different) is the cheerful message of the city's official advertising campaign. *Wien bleibt Wien* (Vienna will always remain Vienna) were the ominous words of Karl Kraus. The truth probably lies – quite typically for Vienna – somewhere between the two.

Theatre and Music

Anyone who mentions theatre in Vienna is usually thinking of the Burgtheater and Max Reinhardt. The fact that a *Piefke* (derogatory word for a German) in the shape of Claus Peymann has been calling the shots since 1986 at the 'Burg', as the theatre is affectionately termed, has left several deep wounds in the Schönbrunn-yellow-coloured mentality of many a Vienna theatregoer. Be that as it may, Mr Peymann (the *Piefke*) has still succeeded in shaking this theatre out of its former complacency. Vienna, by the way, is a city in which the actors at the 'Burg' have the status of civil servants, and premières still provoke scandals—such as Thomas Bernhard's *Heldenplatz*, aimed directly at the darkest recesses of the Viennese soul, or Peter Turrini's *Death and the Devil*, at the première of which state police could be seen scribbling away in the stalls, noting down the bits that might cause offence. Theatre in Vienna is definitely a stimulating experience. There again, small theatre groups are fighting for survival. The Serapionstheater, with its fantastic, pantomime-like theatre collages, deserves a special mention in this category.

As a proud denizen of what is, after all, the 'capital city of music', the Viennese is also concerned about the Opera. And whenever he isn't queueing all night for tickets, equipped with a small folding chair, he's happily sawing away at the legs of the chair belonging to the opera director, who has the most dangerous job in the whole city. The repertoire can vary a great deal in quality, as can the cast – but historic moments do still occur. A useful tip: the best way to get hold of tickets is either to order them in writing from abroad or else discreetly ask the head porter of your hotel. The Opera House only really makes a large profit once a year, by the way: on the night of the Opera Ball, when the city's *jeunesse dorée* waltzes inside the building and the Opera Ball Demo takes place outside on the street. The latter has almost become an institution. And while on the subject of tradition; anyone who likes hearing operetta and goes to the Volksoper is definitely at the right place. Even the city's critics are fond of the Vienna Philharmonic, especially its annual New Year Concert on 1 January in the Great Hall of the Musikverein, which is broadcast right across the world.

Display case at the Burgtheater

Waltzes played in the gardens of Baroque palaces, organ concerts in old churches or classical music and jazz in the Arkadenhof in the Town Hall are all part of the variety provided by the Wiener Musiksommer (July and August), and in May and June the Wiener Festwochen brighten up the cultural life of the city with a programme of international performances ranging from the traditional to the avant-garde. Since the musical *Cats* arrived here, Vienna has thought of itself as home to this particular art-form as well – judge for yourself at the Theater an der Wien.

Of course there's comedy in Vienna too, but it has to be said that it's come back again only recently, because the legendary cabaret scene of the post-war era with Karl Farkas, Ernst Waldbrunn or Helmut Qualtinger has only borne fruit in the last 10 to 15 years or so. Now there are not only young cabaret performers such as Lukas Resetarits, Josef Hader, Erwin Steinhauer or Andreas Vitasek, but also the cabaret venues to go with them, such as the Kulisse, the Metropol, the Spektakel or the Niedermair.

Politics and Population

Ever since universal suffrage was introduced in 1919, Vienna has been ruled by the Social Democrats (SPÖ) with almost 50 per cent of the vote; they were only absent from the Gemeinderat (municipal parliament) between 1934 and 1945. Since the recent elections, the Green party has also been represented in the Town Hall for the first time. Nowhere else is the network of party members so close-woven: of 1.6 million Viennese, 220,000 are members of the SPÖ and 55,000 members of the ÖVP. This does not have to do exclusively with 'red' (SPÖ) and 'black' (ÖVP) political leanings. For a start, you never know just how useful a party membership card can be... For despite all its many promises to the contrary, the state still provides a great deal of jobs on the basis of 'colour' rather than qualifications.

The same goes for the whole of Austria of course, but it's just that Vienna is a bit ahead of everywhere else in this respect. Take the *Freunderlwirtschaft* (Vienna's special version of nepotism), for example: everyone knows a civil servant or a functionary who can get the person in charge of XYZ to do a favour... Karl Kraus speaks of 'going higher up to get things sorted out' in his *Last Days of Humanity*. And the principle still applies today, whether it involves a theatre ticket, building permission or a council flat.

Important laws and decisions get *ausgschnapst* (discussed at a game of cards) before they reach parliament, by the so-called *Sozialpartnerschaft* (the employers' and employees' association). The expression *ausgschnapst* comes from the card game of the same name, and is a highly official term. Here a balance of interests is established without the need to 'bother' the people or their representatives with any problems. True, the employers' and employees' association has brought social peace to Austria and some of the lowest strike figures worldwide, but it has also resulted in a huge amount of shady dealing. 'For some mysterious reason, the Laocoön-like clutches in which all public figures are held bring a black scandal along to match every red one,' as Armin Thurnherr, editor-in-chief of the critical city magazine *Falter*, once accurately put it. There is, so to speak, a 'balance of detection'.

The people have very little say in these matters. And reforms are always introduced from above in Vienna anyway. The Viennese are thoroughly versed in the role of the underdog. It's only when their anger finally boils over that the dam bursts – to everyone's amazement. As Emperor Ferdinand I said in great surprise when the revolution of 1848 broke out: *'Ja derfen's denn des?'* ('But – do they have permission?'). Civic autonomy is only slowly starting to wake up, and is exhausting itself with small protest groups and signature-collecting on issues such as *Baummord* (tree murder) and traffic congestion. The prevailing attitude is usually as follows: there'll be no underground car park in front of *my* house, the traffic can roar through the street next door, etc.

All else that need be said here is that the security officials and police in Vienna have a great deal of power and that the unemployment rate is low; that the city's prisons are the second fullest in Europe (Turkey comes top); and that there are 9,000 associations, 60,000 dogs, around 1,000 *Hofräte* and over 300 sausage stalls. After 10pm every fourth Viennese is already tucked up in bed, though every second one creeps out of it as early as 6am to go to work.

That doesn't have a lot to do with politics, true, more with statistics – but statistics are well-known for the way they sometimes shed light on peculiarities.

Orientation

Although Vienna is clearly laid out, newcomers to the city often have trouble getting their bearings because of the large number of one-way streets. Imagine a huge cake with St Stephen's Cathedral

Inside the Town Hall

towering over it in the middle. Around it are the small streets of District 1 (1. Bezirk), surrounded by the circle of the Ringstrasse and the Donaukanal. Originally, Vienna only occupied today's District 1, and until the 1860s, the city wall followed the course of the Ringstrasse. A Viennese who mentions the *Stadt* (town) usually means District 1.

The large arterial roads then spread out from the Ring in star formation towards the city's outer districts. On the border between what used to be the edge of the city proper and the suburbs runs the second ring around Vienna, the Gürtel, a two-carriageway affair that looks like a ring-road. The so-called *Zweierlinie* (made up of Landesgerichtsstrasse and Lastenstrasse) between the Town Hall and the Karlsplatz runs parallel to the Ring.

If you arrive from the Westautobahn (A1) the best thing to do is to follow the signs saying *Zentrum* (not always easy to spot); this way you reach the Karlsplatz via the Wiental, and then you can go left to the Opera House on the Ring. Here you have to turn off to the left in the direction of the Parlament, because it's a one-way. Only trams are two-way! From the Südautobahn (A2) the best route in is to follow Triesterstrasse as far as the Gürtel, and then go down Schönbrunnerstrasse, which takes you to the Wienzeile just before the Karlsplatz. Anyone coming from the Danube Valley *(Donautal)* – from the Wachau for example – would do best to follow the Nordautobahn (A22) over the Nordbrücke and then go along the Donaukanal as far as Schwedenplatz.

If you're arriving by car from the airport – 17 km (10½ miles) south-east of the city – take the Flughafenautobahn in the direction of the city centre and when you get to the Urania, turn left over the Donaukanal to reach the Ring.

Driving yourself around the city centre is not to be recommended; even the locals get lost regularly in the perpetually-changing maze of one-ways. Kärntnerstrasse, Graben, Kohlmarkt and all the smaller streets around them are pedestrian precincts. Within the Ringstrasse everything can be comfortably reached on foot. The most important sights are all in District 1: along the Ringstrasse are the Opera House, the Parlament, the Burgtheater, the Town Hall, the Alte Universität and Otto Wagner's Post Office Savings Bank, not to mention the Museum of Fine Arts and Natural History, and all of them next to each other.

The two main stations in Vienna are both on the Gürtel: the Südbahnhof at the end of Prinz-Eugen-Strasse, which leads off the Schwarzenbergplatz, and the Westbahnhof, at the end of Mariahilferstrasse.

Vienna is divided up into 23 administrative districts, or *Bezirke*; around the centre are districts 2 to 9, between the Ring and the Gürtel, while districts 10 to 23 are outside the Gürtel. Each district has its own four-digit postal code, with a '1' placed at the beginning of the district's number, and a '0' at the end: eg '1010' would be District 1.

Exploring the City's Heart

From Stephansplatz through the narrow streets of the Old Town to the Opera House. Evening meal at Oswald & Kalb or at Reinhard Gerer's Korso.

– U1/U3 to Stephansplatz –

We'll begin at the heart of the city, or, to be more precise, beneath its heart. Deep down in the U-Bahn station **Stephansplatz**, shortly before the station exit (signposted 'Stephansplatz'), the shiny

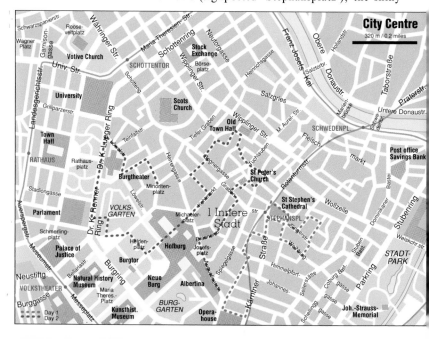

chrome walkway ends in front of a thick wall of glass with the vaulted ceiling of **St Virgil's Chapel** illuminated behind it. Up in the square, pigeons and tourists throng in front of the mighty Cathedral. (Cathedral guided tours: the time of the next tour is posted on a notice-board at the beginning of the left side-aisle.)

The Haas-Haus

The late Romanesque entrance (the so-called *Riesentor* or 'Giant Door') with its wonderful portal is one of the oldest sections of the cathedral, which was consecrated in the year 1147. Towering majestically above its left flank is the 'most finely conceived tower of the Gothic period', the 137-m (450ft) high Südturm, or South Tower, referred to affectionately by the Viennese as the *Steffl*. Access to the Nordturm (North Tower), via lift, is in the left side-aisle (daily 9am–6pm); access to the Südturm on the right outer side of the Cathedral (daily 9am–5.30pm). The Südturm has the better view of Vienna's many rooftop-gardens – if you can brave the flight of 343 narrow steps.

Only two Gothic masterpieces have remained intact inside the triple-naved Cathedral with its Baroque additions: the magnificent Wiener Neustädter Altar (next to the Baroque high altar) and the marvellous pulpit. Under its winding staircase, cathedral sculptor Meister Anton Pilgram immortalised himself in a half-figure self-portrait looking through a window. A few metres further on, a stairway leads down to the **catacombs**. They contain the Herzogsgruft, a vault where the Habsburg family used to preserve their relatives' innards in bronze boxes. Guided tours of the catacombs: Monday to Saturday 10am–11.30am and 1.30pm–4.30pm; Sunday, Public Holidays: 11am–11.30am and 1.30pm–4.30pm.

On the left of the Cathedral, the famous *fiaker* (the name given in Vienna to the horse-drawn cabs as well as to the drivers) are waiting for customers. A trip on these traditional two-horse vehicles can be romantic, but always settle on a fixed price before departure.

On the other side of the Cathedral, on the level of the Churhausgasse, the magnificence of the building is reflected in the round glass facade of the **Haas-Haus**, on the corner of Stephansplatz and the Graben. It's a harmonious mix of Gothic and 20th-century styles. Inside this architectural symphony of colourful marble, shining brass and cool glass, there is a three-storey atrium with expensive shops. From the café on the 7th floor you can get the best view of the Cathedral's colourful roof tiles while you sip morning coffee and enjoy a slice of *Domspitz*, the triangular cake made especially for the establishment with plum jam, poppy seeds and chocolate. Behind the Cathedral, at No 4 Stephansplatz, take the passageway next to the attractive tea-shop Haas & Haas to reach an old-style Viennese inner courtyard: wild vines climb up the dazzlingly white facades, a pergola arches over white wicker furniture; an oasis of tranquillity in the middle of the city. In the courtyard nearby a stone statue between two oleander bushes peers down at the paving-stones. A passageway opposite will lead you to the **Singerstrasse**, via which – having gone past wonderful house facades and the magnificent Baroque palace of Neupauer-Breuner (No 16) – you then turn left into the **Blutgasse**. At the end of the Blutgasse you arrive at the **Domgasse**, a quiet, winding street, where time seems to stand still. Wolfgang Amadeus Mozart used to live at No 5, the **Figaro-Haus** (daily except Monday 9am–12.15pm and 1pm–4.30pm; closed on 1 January, 1 May, 25 December).

If at this stage of the itinerary you feel like a bit of lunch, that archetypal and attractive Viennese establishment known as the **Göttweiger Stiftskeller** is not too far away from here (corner of Seilergasse/Göttweigergasse). The way there leads you along part of the **Kärntnerstrasse**, one of the oldest streets in Vienna. Turned into the city's first pedestrian precinct in 1974, this is *the* place to stroll for locals and tourists alike – with open-air cafés and street-musicians. The Kärntner Durchgang branches off to the right and leads you into the Seilergasse, which in turn opens out on the left into the **Neuer Markt**. This long square, which was once the site of the 'flour market', is lined by elegant patricians' houses. You will see the **Donnerbrunnen**, a Baroque masterpiece, with its scantily-clad figures that once offended the very conservative Empress Maria Theresa. The right-hand corner of the Neuer Markt is dominated by the red-brown facade of the **Kapuzinerkirche** with the **Kaisergruft**, the Habsburg imperial burial vault.

Window display in the Liliengasse

Hot snacks and salads behind a wonderful *Jugendstil* facade can be enjoyed at the **Führich**, in the Führichgasse which leads off the Tegetthoffstrasse, an extension of the Neuer Markt that opens out into a square. Here, sculptor Alfred Hrdlicka erected his *Monument against War and Fascism*.

The Hotel Sacher

On the left-hand side you will see the magnificent **Opera House** (Staatsoper), a structure that was compared by the Viennese to 'an elephant lying down to digest' at its opening in 1869. A mixture of Romanesque, Gothic and Renaissance styles, the building, designed by architects Eduard van der Nüll and August Sicard von Sicardsburg, was not to popular taste. Van der Nüll committed suicide even before the building was opened, and von Siccardsburg died of a broken heart.

Directly opposite the Opera House, the **Albertina** contains the largest collection of graphic art in the world, and the nearby **Albertina Terrace** affords a magnificent view of the green copper roof of the Opera House. Behind the Opera House, in the Philharmonikerstrasse, is the traditional **Hotel Sacher**; it'll send its world-famous cake to you wherever you live.

In the evening you can either indulge in some Viennese *nouvelle cuisine* created by Reinhard Gerer, one of the city's most highly-decorated chefs, in his **Restaurant Korso**, or you can retire to what has become Vienna's best known *Edelbeisl* (old-world tavern), **Oswald & Kalb**. Its comfortable vaulted room in the Bäckerstrasse is a meeting-place for writers, politicians and artists. House specialities are *Gefüllte Kalbsbrust* (stuffed veal brisket), *Tafelspitz* (boiled fillet of beef) or *Wiener Schnitzel*.

The courtyard at Haas & Haas

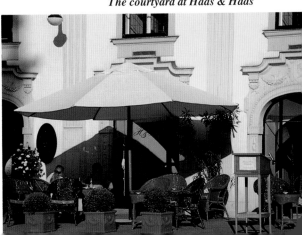

Imperial Vienna

A stroll through the Vienna of the Habsburgs, the Romans and the Babenbergs; to a traditional pastry shop and café; evening meal in an old-fashioned Viennese 'Edelbeisl', and a nightcap in Vienna's finest 'Plüschbar'.

– U3 to Herrengasse or taxi to Ballhausplatz or Minoritenplatz –

Only a few steps away from the bustling business streets of the city, the **Minoritenplatz** is a tranquil oasis where all one can hear is the sound of footsteps resounding on its cobblestones. In the centre of the square is the 700-year-old Basilica of the Minorites which gave it its name. In the direction of the Heldenplatz you can see the rear of **Ballhausplatz**. The magnificent Federal Chancellery building on this square was constructed in 1717 by Lukas von Hildebrandt; Metternich once used to pull his political strings here, and the Congress of Vienna also took place within its walls.

Leave the Ballhausplatz on your right and enter the spacious Heldenplatz in front of the **Hofburg**, the former centre of imperial power and government, sadly recently damaged by fire. The equestrian statues of Prince Eugene and Archduke Karl dominate the square. The statue of Karl is the only one in the world to have its full weight resting on just one hoof; throughout his lifetime, the sculptor had nightmares that it might fall over. At the front end of the Heldenplatz is the majestic **Neue Burg**, with the National-bibliothek (National Library) behind its immense colonnade.

Now you must follow the clattering hooves of the *fiakers* over to the left and through the entry gate into the Hofburg. On the right

Fiaker on the Heldenplatz

you will see the oldest part, the **Alte Burg** (or Old Palace). The magnificent dark-red portal leads to the Swiss Court, or Schweizer Hof, and the Treasury (Schatzkammer), where the 1,000-year-old imperial crown of the Holy Roman Empire was displayed – the Treasury is undergoing repairs.

Go past the Reichskanzleitrakt, the seat of the Federal President, and the next gateway will lead you into the Michaelertrakt, crowned by the impressive Michaeler Dome. The sun's rays pierce the round windows of the dome and bathe the passageway, with its creamy-white stucco and magnificent statues, in a mysterious light. To the right, a stairway leads up to the former Imperial Chambers.

The Demel confectionery

Now you step out of the Hofburg into the Michaelerplatz. The remains of ancient walls, dating back to Vienna's Roman past, were discovered in its centre at the beginning of the 1990s. On the left is the resurrected **Café Griensteidl**, which does excellent breakfasts.

Opposite the Michaeler Dome, the pedestrian precinct of the **Kohlmarkt** begins, flanked by the **Michaelerkirche** and the **Loos-Haus**. This latter building, constructed by Adolf Loos in 1911, was mocked by the Viennese as a 'house without eyebrows' (because the windows didn't have lintels) and a 'marble coal scuttle'; the Emperor in the Hofburg opposite, out of protest at the 'unbearable sight', is even said to have shifted his office to other rooms. Today the Loos-Haus is considered a milestone of modern architecture.

The Kohlmarkt is one of the most elegant shopping streets in the city. Shops belonging to former *k.u.k. Hoflieferanten* ('purveyors to the Imperial Court') throng the sides of the street. After passing the *Kammeruhrmacher* (imperial watchmaker) Franz Morawetz and the elegant displays of Christofle and Kiss & Rosza, you will come face-to-face with a Viennese institution: the **Hofkonditorei Demel** – a traditional pastry shop in its purest form, with black-clad waitresses, called *Demelinerinnen*, who address their guests in the third person. The interior contains all manner of fine confectionery: cakes, wonderfully packed sweets, delicious specialities. At the end of the 1980s the Demel had a spot of unwelcome publicity because of its owner at that time, the designer Udo Proksch, and his ship, the *Lucona*, which sank under mysterious circumstances. These days – much to the horror of tradition-conscious Viennese – it belongs to a German industrialist. But if you want to soak up the atmosphere of Vienna's imperial past then this is the place to do it.

A few steps further on and you reach Retti, the candle shop, and Schullin the jewellers, both designed by Hans Hollein and for a long time the only buildings in Vienna by this internationally renowned architect. At the corner of Kohlmarkt and Wallnerstrasse it's worth taking a look at the shop belonging to the **Gebrüder Thonet**, who made furniture history with their *Bugholzsessel*, a kind of bent wooden armchair. Anyone whose tummy is not already full of Demel cake and who feels like a little snack will find he's come to the right place at the **Levant**, only a few metres further on, with its assortment of Levantine vegetable dishes and crunchy doner sandwiches.

A few metres further on you should turn right into the Haarhof, an old and narrow Viennese street which will take you past the ultra-traditional Esterhazy-Keller and up to the **Naglergasse**. This picturesque street with its fine old burghers' houses – No 13 is particularly attractive – winds its way along what once used to be the south-western flank of the Roman garrison of Vindobona.

Opposite the point where the Haarhof leads into the Naglergasse is the square known as **am Hof**, once the centre of the Babenberg kingdom and the second oldest square in Vienna. Opposite the Church of the Nine Choirs of Angels stands the Kattus-Haus, one of the oldest houses in Vienna, and next to it at No 10 the magnificent former Arsenal (*Zeughaus*) which today is the headquarters of the city's fire brigade. Next to the church, a narrow passageway leads off to the right into the **Schulhof**; down here you'll find a genuine piece of old Vienna, its silence only broken now and then by the clip-clop of a *fiaker*.

Soloist near the Graben

At No 2 is the city's Uhrenmuseum (Horological Museum), while in the old palace at No 4 there is the delightful Puppen- und Spielzeugmuseum (Doll and Toy Museum).

After going left along the Parisergasse you will reach the **Judenplatz**. The most imposing of all the magnificent buildings lining this square is the former **Bohemian Chancellery** at No 11, the work of Baroque master builder Johann Bernhard Fischer von Erlach, and today the seat of the Austrian Constitutional Court. Anyone with a sudden craving for Italian *antipasti* can sample the wares at **Da Conte** directly opposite. Those who prefer more substantial Viennese country cooking will enjoy the **Ofenloch** in the adjacent Kurrentgasse. Don't forget to take a swift look at the charmingly overgrown inner courtyard of house No 12 as you go by.

Next to this house, a passageway leads off to the left into the winding, horseshoe-shaped Kleeblattgasse and onward to the Tuchlauben. Here you should definitely take a quick look at the *Neidhardt Frescoes*, Vienna's oldest profane wall-paintings, at No 19.

From here we turn right into the Bauernmarkt and continue through the Trattnerhof to the **Graben**, which is closed to traffic. Street-musicians gather around the Plague Column (*Pestsäule*) and in the numerous *Schanigärten* (outdoor pub-gardens). At No 11 is the magnificent Baroque palace of **Bartolotti-Partenfeld**, one of the last pre-*Gründerzeit* burgher's houses in the Graben, with its imposing domed roof. If you fancy a more savoury snack turn into the Dorotheergasse and enter the traditional sandwich restaurant with the name of Tresniewski for a highly-seasoned mini-baguette and a *Pfiff* (an eighth of a litre) of beer. Opposite this establishment is the incarnation of the Viennese coffee-house *par excellence*: the **Café Hawelka**. After a final look at the magnificent roof figures on the house at the corner of the Graben and the Kohlmarkt you should leave the pedestrian precinct and turn left into the Habsburgergasse, which leads you back to the Hofburg. On the left-hand side is the **Stallburg**, one of Vienna's finest Renaissance edifices, with a marvellous *Arkadenhof* (arcaded courtyard). Originally built for the Emperor Maximilian, the building was later used as the imperial stables. Today it houses the Lipizzaner horses belonging to the world-famous Spanische Reitschule, or **Spanish Riding School**. The morning training can be viewed Tuesday to Saturday from 10am–noon, from February to June and September to mid-December (no reservations necessary); however, tickets for the performances have to be applied for in writing months in advance!

Directly opposite the Stallburg and to the right is the Josefsplatz with its baroque **Winter Riding School**, and a few steps further on, the **Augustinerkirche**. It was here that the Emperor Franz Joseph married his beloved Sissy, and it also contains a highly macabre speciality: the **Loretto Chapel** containing the *Herzgruft* (not to be confused with the Cathedral's *Herzogsgruft*), a vault where the Habsburgs preserved their ancestors' hearts in silver containers…

In the evening head for the **Pfudl** in the Bäckerstrasse. In a really traditional country atmosphere, vast helpings of traditional Vienna home cooking are served, such as *Zwiebelrostbraten* (fried beef and onion), or *Beuschel* (cooked heart, lung, liver and sweetbreads of a calf, thinly sliced and served in a savoury sauce). To round off the day, how about a touch of Viennese elegance? A nightcap in the cosy half-darkness of the **Eden**. This is the most traditional *Plüschbar* in Vienna, and men have to wear a tie to get in.

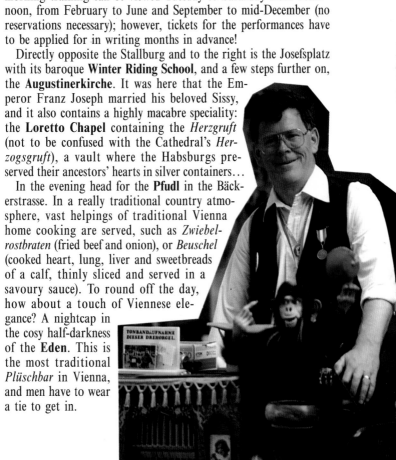

3. The Old City

To the Old City between the Schwedenplatz and the Hoher Markt; then along the narrow streets of the Bermuda Triangle to the Jugendstil jewel Ankeruhr (Anchor Clock); Otto Wagner's Post Office Savings Bank. Evening meal in Salzamt.

– U1, U4, tram numbers 1 or 2, or taxi to Schwedenplatz –

The **Schwedenplatz**, on the Donaukanal, borders the oldest section of Vienna. After you emerge from the U-Bahn station exit you go uphill, up the steep **Griechengasse**, which takes you straight to a fine example of Old Vienna. Medieval houses stand to the right and left, and a rusty sign warns: *Achtung Fuhrwerke* (Beware of horse-drawn vehicles). Just before the end of the narrow street there is a passageway on the left leading to the **Griechenbeisl** (Greeks' Tavern), an establishment once frequented by Beethoven, Schubert and Strauss. It was from the – nowadays very touristy – Griechenbeisl that the famous Pilsner Urquell beer once used to be exported around the world. As you head for the historical rooms of this dark wood-panelled tavern, don't be frightened if you suddenly get your foot caught in a grating set into the ground with a life-sized dummy sitting beneath it: the **Lieber Augustin**. This legendary typically Viennese figure once toured the city's streets as a ballad-singer. He became famous one night when, drunk and singing, he fell down a sewer…

Having passed the Lieber Augustin and three Turkish cannon balls embedded in the wall that were discovered during renovation work in the 1960s, you climb a wooden spiral staircase to a Gothic Tower-house: each floor has an idyllic-looking balcony full of lovingly-tended plants. Now return to the Griechengasse which leads directly into the **Fleischmarkt**. Almost immediately you will see the magnificent facade of No 13, the **Greek Church**, right next to the Griechenbeisl; No 15,

The Old City

320 m / 0.2 miles

Leopoldsgasse
Rotensterngasse
Zirkusgasse
Schmelzgasse
NESTROYPLATZ
Danube Canal
Obere Donaustr.
Holandstr.
Franz Josefs-Kai
Salztorbr.
Taborstraße
Praterstraße
Donaustr.
Salzgries
Morzin-platz
Marien-brücke
Schweden-brücke
Untere
Aspernbrücke
Donaustr.
Urania
Hoher Markt
Fleisch-
SCHWEDENPL.
Joh. Raab-Platz
Radetzky-str.
markt
Post office Savings Bank
Rotenturmstr.
Bäcker
Stubenring
Vordere Zollamtstr.
Wollzeile
Dominikaner
STEPHANSPL.
Singerstr.
Museum of Applied Art
Mariengasse
Weihburggasse
Stuben
Bast.
DR. K. LUEGER-PLATZ
Weiskirch.str.
Central Station
STADT-PARK
Parkring
Invalidenstr.
Sellerstätte
LANDSTR.

● ● ● Day 3

The facade of the Roter Engel

the **Schwindhof**, built in 1718 and the birthplace of the painter Moritz von Schwind, is also worth a visit. From the Griechenbeisl, turn right and make your way past the ivy-covered **Marhold** inn – which is a very good tip for anyone keen on substantial Viennese food. Only a few steps further on, in the inner courtyard of house No 16, is the enticing **Siddharta** restaurant, the local hero among Vienna's vegetarian restaurants.

In the direction of Rotenturmstrasse there are fashionable boutiques, the Atelier at No 16, and the elegant arcade belonging to Kapuzina, plus sophisticated fashion at Emis. The right-hand side of the street is dominated by the facades of old shop buildings dating from the 1920s: the original branch office of the Julius Meinl trading company, for example, opposite No 16. Next to it there's the original copper facade of the BAWAG-Haus. At the corner of Rotgasse, the stylishly-designed **K2** serves the best *sushi* in town.

Opposite, the Rabensteig takes you down into the middle of the so-called **Bermuda Triangle**. This area between the Rabensteig, Seitenstettengasse and the Ruprechtskirche is where the restaurant boom at the end of the 1970s had its roots. The name comes from the large number of people who've lost their way while spending long nights touring the restaurants and pubs in the area. At the end of the Rabensteig, at No 5, is the **Roter Engel**. This pub, designed by the Vienna architectural partnership Coop Himmelblau, is considered to be the real heart of the Bermuda Triangle, along with the beer paradise called **Krah Krah** opposite.

Next to the Rote Engel, the Seitenstettengasse winds its way up to the Ruprechtsplatz. At No 2 is the **synagogue** built in 1826 by Biedermeier architect Josef Kornhäusl, with its magnificent oval interior; it is the only synagogue to have survived the Nazis' wave of destruction. A few metres further on you will enter the **Ruprechtsplatz** proper. On the left, on the steps leading down to the Fleischmarkt, is the **Kornhäuselturm**, a tower-like house in the Biedermeier style, where Adalbert Stifter observed the total eclipse of the sun in the year 1842.

The Ruprechtsplatz contains several original fashion shops as well as the **Salzamt**, star of the Vienna restaurant scene, and my recommendation for your dinner this evening. Directly opposite it is the romantically overgrown **Ruprechtskirche**, the oldest church in Vienna. But now go back to the Ruprechtsplatz and turn right into the **Sterngasse**. The shop on the corner called Firis contains fashions by Romeo Gigli and Katherine Hamnett, at No 2 you can see the Shakespeare & Company English bookstore, and next to it the Finstere Stern, the finest wine store in Vienna.

At the end of the Sterngasse a staircase leads down to the Marc-Aurel-Strasse – to the right is one of Vienna's 'in' cafés, the **Salz-**

The Anchor Clock

gries. Directly opposite, the old Salvatorgasse leads to Stoss im Himmel leading to Wipplingerstrasse, where a magnificent **patrician's house**, which was used as the Town Hall until 1885, can be seen at No 8; opposite is the richly-decorated rear facade of the former Bohemian Chancellery.

Going down Wipplingerstrasse to the left brings you to the **Hohe Markt**, the oldest market-place in Vienna. Standing in its centre is the **Vermählungsbrunnen** (Marriage Fountain), built by the son of Baroque architect Johann Bernhard Fischer von Erlach in 1732. Garda at No 4 is the right place for ice-cream fans, and a few metres further on, at No 3, Roman excavations can be visited. Groups of tourists assemble hourly in front of the **Ankeruhr** (Anchor Clock). This clock, a *Jugendstil* jewel, was completed in 1914 and spans houses 10 and 11 like a bridge. Each time it strikes the hour it displays a different Viennese historical figure, from Roman emperor Marcus Aurelius to composer Joseph Haydn. At noon all 12 of the figures can be observed wandering by to musical accompaniment.

Jesuitengasse

At the end of the Hohe Markt you must cross the Rotenturmstrasse again and via the Lugeck enter the 'gateway' to the **Bäckerstrassenviertel** (Bäckerstrasse Quarter), another popular pub area. At No 1 Lugeck, gorgeous *belle époque* furniture by Otto Wagner and Joseph Hoffmann can be seen in the shop-window-like displays of the Galerie Ambiente. The Bäckerstrasse forks away to the right, and a colourful relief marks the way to the *Schnitzelkönig* (Schnitzel King) **Figlmüller** famed for gigantic portions of *Schnitzel*. For the time being you must stay on the left-hand side of the street, though, and stroll down the Sonnenfelsgasse with its lovingly restored old houses; at No 12, steps lead down to the **Zwölf-Apostel Keller** wine bar, much frequented by students, and at No 9, looking discreet, is **Josefine**, the noblest brothel in Vienna; next to it, **Die Bar** attracts scores of night revellers.

Turn left into the small Schönlaterngasse where a passageway at No 5 leads to the magnificent **Heiligenkreuzerhof**. This courtyard is largely medieval, and a Kunsthandwerksmarkt (craft fair) brings the old walls here to life once a month. At the end of the Heiligenkreuzerhof you will come into the small Grashofgasse, and via the Köllnerhofgasse return to the Fleischmarkt again. Passing the main Post Office at No 19 (open 24 hours a day), you now branch off to the left into the narrow Postgasse, and a few metres further on, down the Auwinkel as far as the Dominikanerbastei, where you will see the rear of Otto Wagner's **Post Office Savings Bank**. Passing some elegant burghers' houses, you then go along Wiesingerstrasse, and turn right down Biberstrasse to reach the building's main entrance on the Georg-Coch-Platz.

Built in 1906, it is one of the main works of *Jugendstil* architect Otto Wagner and with its marble-slab and aluminium facade was the first 'modern' building on the Ringstrasse – a prime example of architecture during the Vienna Secession, which tried to combine a strict, matter-of-fact approach with decorative flourishes. The spacious hall is distinctive for its elegant functionalism, and it contains some of the furniture originally designed by Otto Wagner.

For lunch, try **Hedrich**, at 2 Stubenring. This small restaurant, run by top cook Richard Hedrich, is the favourite lunchtime destination of many of the civil servants from the ministry nearby. Afterwards walk a short way along the Ringstrasse past the Stadtpark to Dr. Karl-Lueger-Platz, where you should have coffee in the 50s-style **Café Prückel**. Evening is the best time to get lost in the Bermuda Triangle, where you can try the **Krah Krah**, the **Rote Engel** or the **Salzamt** restaurant.

Detail of the entrance to the Figlmüller restaurant

1. Parks, Parliament and Palaces

From the Parlament to the Burgtheater, past the elegant palaces on the Freyung to the ancient church of Maria am Gestade.

– U3 to Volkstheater –

The Volksgarten U-Bahn exit leads directly to the park of the same name on the **Ringstrasse**. On the other side of the road is the majestic **Parlament**, built in the last century in Greek Revival style.

Enter the Volksgarten from the side that faces the Heldenplatz. Straight away on the right you will see the enticing-looking **Meierei**, a small garden pavilion with a Schanigarten, where it is possible to enjoy delicious breakfasts in the summer. Between the trees you should be able to make out the columns of the Theseustempel, a favourite meeting-place with the young. A few metres further on there are rows of rose bushes in front of geometrically laid-out flowerbeds. Lots of graceful-looking wrought-iron chairs are lined up here to greet visitors, who can sit and sun themselves and watch the figures on the roof of the Parlament building playing hide-and-seek in the tree-tops across in the direction of the Ring.

Leave the park and head for the **Burgtheater**. 'The St Peter's of world theatre' – as this imperial theatre was once described by Rolf Hochhuth – is a mighty round building in Italian Renaissance style. Today it continues to brag – almost obsessively – about its commanding role in the German-speaking theatrical world.

Opposite the Burgtheater is the imposing-looking **Town Hall** (Rathaus). The most distinctive feature of this building, with its neo-Gothic towers, arcades and courtyards, is its famous 3.4m (11ft) high *Rathausmann*. It's

Monument in front of the parliament

worth taking a brief stroll at this point through the idyllic **Rathauspark**, with its huge and ancient trees. Then it's time to cross the Ring once again, in the direction of the theatre. Here, right next to the Burgtheater, a stopover at the highly traditional **Café Landtmann**

The Rathausplatz and Burgtheater

is an absolute must. Its spacious rooms and huge terrace are a favourite meeting place for a colourful assortment of journalists and party functionaries. From here, continue on up the Ring a short way and then turn right down the Schreyvogelgasse. A few steps further and a steep path leads up to No 10, the **Dreimäderlhaus**, dating from the Biedermeier period. From here you have a good view of the Ringstrasse and the magnificent Alte Universität.

At the end of the Schreyvogelgasse turn right into the **Mölkerbastei**, part of the city's former fortifications. The **Pasqualatihaus** at No 8 is one of many places where Beethoven lived. Make a short detour back to the Dreimäderlhaus, then go left through narrow streets over the Mölkersteig and down to the Schottengasse.

Directly opposite, a passageway leads from No 2 Helfersdorferstrasse, to the Schottenhof: framed by the walls of the monastery that the Babenbergs built in 1155, the shady garden of the dignified **Café Haag** is very attractive in the summer. At the end of the Schottenhof, another passageway leads to the Freyung. On the left is the **Schottenkirche**, and opposite is the **Palais Harrach**, which has been crumbling away for years and is in urgent need of repair. Haydn's mother was once the family cook there. Opposite the Schottenkirche (Scots' Church) is the magnificent **Palais Kinski**, which you pass on the left in order to go down the Herrengasse.

At No 17 is the attractive shopping arcade of the **Palais Ferstel** – a fine ensemble consisting of brass, glass and marble, crowned by the magnificent **Donaunixen Fountain**. Turn right for one of Vienna's most traditional coffee-houses, the **Central**. The main entrance is on the corner of Herrengasse and Strauchgasse. A dummy

of *Kaffeehausliterat* Peter Altenburg is slouched here, looking rather lost among all the shining tables and windows. For lunch, a good place to go is the **Bistrot** in the middle of the Ferstel-Passage. At the end of this arcade you step into the **Freyung**. It was in this triangular square in 1987, while an underground car-park was being built, that parts of the 1156 Babenburg fortress were discovered.

At traffic-lights at the end of the Freyung, Tiefer Graben leads off downhill to the left. At No 8 is yet another Beethoven-lived-here house. From here you reach the **Hohe Brücke**. Once the site of the western gate in Roman times, today a magnificent *Jugendstil* stairway leads *zum Glücke* (literally, 'to happiness'), ie up to the Glücksspielstelle (casino) in Wipplingerstrasse. Stay in the Tiefer Graben, however, and go on a little bit further to No 32, with its reddish facade. This is the high-class brothel known as the **Orient Hotel**, which also contains the finest *Plüschbar* in all Vienna.

At the end of Tiefer Graben a stairway leads upwards to Am Gestade. One level higher up is the majestic 14th-century church of **Maria am Gestade** with its enormously high Gothic windows and a marvellous Gothic helm roof above the entrance on its left-hand side. A lot of trendy pubs and bars have sprung up on the Passauerplatz around the church. Before you mingle with the crowds in the **Garibaldi** on Schwertstrasse, look at the impressive Baroque portal, decorated with stone figures, to the left of the entrance.

Inside the Café Central

2. Jugendstil and Markets

Otto Wagner's Jugendstil and the Vienna Secession; a stroll around the Naschmarkt, the Flea Market and the Art and Antiques market by the Donaukanal.

– U1, U2, U4 to Karlsplatz –

Pure Jugendstil: The Secession

The **Otto Wagner Pavilion** stands in the middle of the Karlsplatz like a memorial in an architectural desert. To get a good look at this *Jugendstil* (art nouveau) jewel, which was built for the Vienna municipal railway at the turn of the century, take the Resselpark/Karlsplatz exit from the U-Bahn arcade and then head 'underground' once again – for this square with its innumerable crossroads is not only a town planning disaster, but is also hell for pedestrians.

Wander along underground until you reach the entrance marked 'Sezession', which leads directly to this temple of Viennese *Jugendstil. Krauthappl* ('the cabbage') is the nickname given by the Viennese to the cupola of golden laurel leaves on top of the snow-white **Secession Building**. Above the entrance to the exhibition hall, built in 1897, fine gold letters form the inscription: *Der Zeit ihre Kunst, der Kunst ihre Freiheit* (To every age its art, to art its freedom). With the foundation of the Vienna Secession, the group of artists that included Gustav Klimt and Otto Wagner became the fathers of Viennese *Jugendstil*. Gustav Klimt's 34-m (111-ft) long **Beethoven Frieze** has been on display downstairs here since 1986 – it is a very rich interpretation of the composer's ninth symphony in visual terms. The small and colourfully decorated café-bar in the basement is a good place for a short coffee break (the entrance is in the rear facade of the building).

From the Secession Building you turn right and cross the Getreidemarkt to the beginning of the Linke Wienzeile and also the **Naschmarkt**, the so-called 'belly of Vienna'. This, Vienna's largest market, was built in 1916 above the Wien River. Mountains of citrus fruit, Arabian spices, Turkish bread and horseflesh are piled high in this almost 500-m (1,600-ft) long market. Hawkers and 150 permanent stalls lend the whole place the atmosphere of a Viennese-Levantine bazaar. Just let yourself be carried along – you'll be sure to find all you bargained for and more besides. And on the subject of bargains: the further the stalls are from the city centre, the cheaper they generally are. Don't forget to glance over at Otto Wagner's magnificent *Jugendstil* building the **Majolikahaus**, and its

39

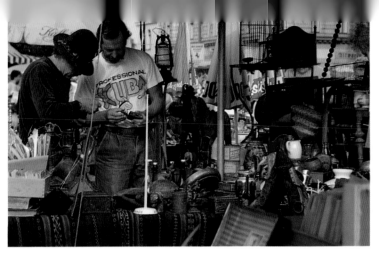

The Saturday flea market behind the station

neighbour with the gold-decorated facade by Kolo Moser.

At the end of the Naschmarkt, behind the Otto Wagner station building in the Kettenbrückengasse there is a **flea market** every Saturday. A talent for hard bargaining combined with luck is a real necessity here, however, if you want to find a nice old antique among the knick-nacks, old clothing and prohibitively expensive lamps doing their best to look *Jugendstil*. The same rules apply here as to all flea markets the world over: come in the morning, and keep a close watch on your wallet.

At the end of the flea market on the left is the **Brauneis** restaurant (2 Hamburgerstrasse). Those in the know avoid this old-fashioned original Viennese tavern on Saturdays, preferring to come on Wednesdays which is *Schnitzeltag*, Schnitzel-day. Otherwise, the best thing to do is to go back to the Kettenbrückengasse; at No 9 the **Goldene Glocke**, with its fine Viennese cuisine and carefully-tended garden, awaits you.

Another open-air market is held at weekends on the Donaukanal, but the **Art and Antiques Market** is a far less professionally-run affair – which is actually a very good thing. The best way to get there is to take the U4 at the Kettenbrückengasse in the direction of Heiligenstadt, get out at Schottenring and then turn left before the Salztorbrücke down in the direction of the Donaukanal. Improvised open-air stalls offer old books, granny's silver, faded postcards. The food here is rather touristy, but on a fine summer's day that can easily be ignored as you sip a refreshing drink at the Riverside Bakery or afloat on the *Johann Strauss*.

You can also save your trip to the Donaukanal market for a Sunday, and perhaps combine it with a short round trip on a boat. Behind the *Jugendstil* Stadtpark station building a magnificent flight of steps leads you down to the Wien River, which at this point is not built up. Stroll through the marvellous park laid out in memory of the 'waltz king' Johann Strauss. The imposing-looking bronze statue with its marble relief symbolising the Blue Danube waltz is one of the most-photographed sights of Vienna.

From the Opera House, along the Kärntnerstrasse and the Himmelpfortgasse.

– U4, U1 to Karlsplatz, trams 1,2, J as far as the Opera House –

Starting behind the **Vienna State Opera House**, which is so reminiscent of an Italian Renaissance palazzo, is the city's oldest pedestrian precinct: the **Kärntnerstrasse**. Lined with long-established shops and enlivened by *Schanigärten* (outdoor pub gardens) and street musicians, this stretch of street is Vienna's number one place for a stroll.

To start off with make a quick visit to No 38, **Tourist Information**, where maps of the city and a monthly guide to what's on can be collected free of charge. A few steps further on, the world-famous *Sachertorte* is on sale. Before joining the throng of shoppers, the Malteserkirche opposite deserves a quick detour; then you can start. Pass No 41, the salon belonging to the late doyen of Viennese haute couture Fred Adlmüller, where generations of politicians' wives and high-society ladies have bought their ballroom dresses, and then there's Willi Silbernagel for international men's fashions at No 13. Next door there's elegant porcelain at Wahliss. On the upper floors of Lobmeyer (No 26) there is a glass museum, with fine examples of old tableware. Anyone who'd rather remain in the epoch of Josef Hoffmann and the *Wiener Werkstätte* should go next to Backhausen (on the corner of the Johannisgasse). As well as featuring expensive materials from all over the world, this establishment also specialises in elegant textiles of turn-of-the-century design. You have to go up to the first floor, though – the ground floor has a ticket-counter and is stuffed with touristy knick-knacks. If you are feeling peckish, visit the *Imperial Konditorei* (pastry shop) called Heiner at No 21 – the range of delicious cakes there is irresistible.

Now you must stroll a little further along the Kärntnerstrasse and then turn right into the attractive Himmelpfortgasse. A few metres further on go left into Rauhensteingasse, to Alexander, a beautifully styled fashion shop. Then return to the Himmelpfortgasse, where at No 6 you will find the oldest coffee-house in Vienna, the **Frauenhuber**, which used to be a restaurant owned by the Empress Maria Theresa's personal chef. It's a great place for coffee or lunch. Right beside the café is a magnificent Baroque burgher's house, its first floor decorated lavishly with angels.

A few steps further on at No 9, k.u.k. Kuriositäten sells old postcards, badges and mugs painted with the Emperor's portrait. Part of the Finance Ministry resides at No 8 opposite, in Prince Eugene's magnificent former Winterpalais. Good second-hand clothes and antiques can be found a few steps further on at No 11 Partout, while the Galerie Slavik at No 15 is very interesting architecturally. Notice the artistically designed shop signs above some of the portals on the left-hand side of the street.

This walk ends at the point where the Himmelpfortgasse reaches the Seilerstätte. On the way back it's worth trying some of the smaller streets that run parallel to the Kärntnerstrasse; or you may have worked up an appetite, in which case head back to the **Frauenhuber** for a very Viennese lunch.

4. The Spittelberg

A stroll through the Spittelberg, the Biedermeier Quarter, to the smallest home in Vienna.

– U2, U3 or taxi to the Volkstheater –

The Messepalast U-Bahn exit leads right to the middle of the Baroque ensemble that was built by Johann Bernhard Fischer von Erlach and housed the **Imperial Stables** for 200 years. This magnificent building with its spacious inner courtyards is now to be turned into a huge museum.

Cross the Burggasse and stroll past the **Volkstheater** before turning right into Museumsstrasse, where old UFA films are screened at the tiny **Bellaria** cinema. Turn left into the Neustiftgasse, where the traditional inn at No 15, **Anna Rippel**, does excellent Viennese home cooking. Directly opposite, the small Mechitaristengasse leads to the monastery of the Armenian Mechitarists, hidden behind an unremarkable facade at No 6. A little further on turn left into Lerchenfelderstrasse. No 13 is one of the finest old *Durchhäuser* (arch-connected houses) in Vienna; the many courtyards succeed one another under church-like round arches, and the perspective changes with every new step, until you finally come out into the Neustiftgasse again. Directly opposite, at No 19, the monks' own brand of Benedictine, a liqueur called Mechitarine, is on sale.

A few steps further on you will arrive at the **Ulrichsplatz** on the left. If you go left round the back of the church of the same name you will be confronted by a fine row of tiny Baroque houses all huddled together, with romantic inner courtyards; house No 2, built in the 19th century, is particularly delightful. There's a fine rustic pub next door, the **Spatzennest**, with its own very cosy *Schanigarten* (pub garden).

The nearby Burggasse has unfortunately become the 'motorway' of District 7. The fine old portal of the Bäckerei Zöchling on the corner of Burggasse and Sigmundgasse deserves attention, though. Passing original and sometimes very dusty old junk shops, you approach the **Spittelberg**. The Biedermeier house at No 13 is particularly delightful, and a two-floor restaurant there serves traditional Viennese delicacies such as *Rostbraten* (pan-fried sirloin steak) or *Kaiserschöberlsuppe*. Between the 18th and 19th centuries this Baroque and Biedermeier quarter was regarded as a sinful, evil redlight district, with one notorious brothel next to the other. Saved from collapse in the 1970s, the Spittelberg today is a fine example of successful urban renovation.

From the Burggasse you turn right into the Spittelberg's 'high street', the Spittelberggasse, which is closed to cars. The charming house on the corner, Zum Schwarzen Mohren ('The Black Moor'), contains the Bohème pub. As you continue, small galleries, cafés and craft shops will greet you almost every step of the way, as will historic plaques on the magnificently decorated facades, all of which have a story to relate: house No 22 is called Zum Heiligen Christoph ('St Christopher's') and No 18 Zum Schwarzen Bären ('The Black Bear').

People meet here in the little square in front of the splashing fountain for a *crêpe* or one of the very healthy and also very expensive vegetarian dishes served by the **Creperie am Spittelberg**. The monthly *Kunsthandwerksmarkt* (Craft Fair) here attracts a lot of visitors, as do the many *Schanigärten* in the summertime. Rents here have become exorbitant for former inhabitants, and the plan to make the area attractive to young artists has never really materialised; nevertheless this quarter, with its narrow streets and won-

derful little houses, is a real eye-opener for those who enjoy a feel of the past, and who like to dream of Old Vienna.

Anyone who finds the pubs here too pretentious and expensive would be well advised to meet up at the **Amerlingbeisl** at No 8 Stiftgasse, a street that runs parallel. The inner courtyard of the small Baroque house called Zu den drei Herzen (The Three Hearts), overgrown with greenery, does superb breakfasts and suppers, and the coffee is excellent.

You now go uphill a little way along the Stiftgasse until you reach

On the Spittelberg

the Siebensterngasse. To your right is a long row of antique shops all clustered together, each with a fine assortment of *Jugendstil* items, and to your left, the Siebensterngasse leads down to the Kirchberggasse. Behind the decrepit door at No 16 there is an enchanting overgrown garden among crumbling walls, which leads you through to the Siebensterngasse. Opposite, on the corner of Breitegasse and Burggasse, you can admire the smallest house in Vienna: built in 1872, it now contains a jewellery shop.

Return to the Messepalast via the Burggasse. Opposite are the majestic figures on the roof of the **Naturhistorisches Museum** (Natural History Museum), and to the right, the magnificent dome of the **Kunsthistorisches Museum** (Museum of Fine Arts).

5. Belvedere and the Baroque

A walk from the Karlskirche to the Belvedere via the Schwarzenberg Palace.

– U1, U2, U4 to Karlsplatz –

At the beginning of the 1970s, Alain Delon and Burt Lancaster took part in a breathtaking chase sequence in the film *Scorpio*, which was filmed in the huge hole in the ground made during construction work on the **Karlsplatz** U-Bahn station; today the site lies under the grass of the tiny Ressel Park. Only a few steps across the park from the U-Bahn station of the same name is the **Karlskirche**, one of the most important Baroque buildings in Europe. This church, built in 1722, with its 72-m (235-ft) high dome and mighty columns looks almost oriental – a sort of mix between St Peter's in Rome and Hagia Sophia in Istanbul. When Emperor Charles VI laid the foundation stone on a small rise here, the

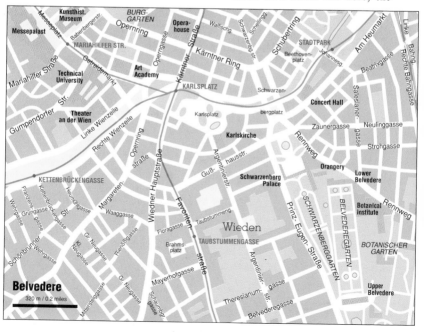

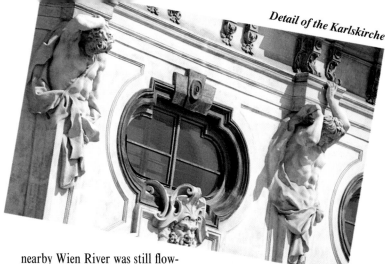

nearby Wien River was still flow-
ing freely. The open space that the church was
meant to have in front of it has fallen victim to modern town
planning, and the small pond with its Henry Moore Sculpture in
front of the Karlskirche is a rather weak apologia. But don't let
that spoil your enjoyment of this masterpiece of the Baroque.

From the Karlskirche you turn right, passing the **Historisches
Museum der Stadt Wien**, until we reach the Schwarzenbergplatz
with its fountain, the Hochstrahlbrunnen. If you walk a short way
down Prinz-Eugen-Strasse you'll find yourself in front of the entrance to the magnificent **Schwarzenberg Palace**. This masterpiece
was the work of Baroque architects Lukas von Hildebrandt and Johann Bernhard Fischer von Erlach. From the Palais Restaurant
and the Nobelhotel situated in the right wing of the building you
can get a superb view of the grand private park.

You now go back to Schwarzenbergplatz and turn right into
Rennweg. At No 6 is the entrance to the park surrounding the
Belvedere, one of the most magnificent Baroque palaces in Europe.
In 1714, Prince Eugene of Savoy had a summer palace built in
front of the gates of the city of that time, and today it is considered the chief and best work of Lukas von Hildebrandt. Right at
the Rennweg entrance you will see the **Lower Belvedere**, which today houses Vienna's **Baroque Museum**.

From the Lower Belvedere, a walk through a 500-m (1,600-ft)
long French garden leads to the **Upper Belvedere**. This summer
residence was built in 1721, and was used for official receptions. At
the beginning of this century it was the home of the Archduke
Franz Ferdinand, the heir to the Austrian throne, whose murder in
Sarajevo sparked the beginning of World War I, and in 1955 the
Austrian State Treaty was signed in the red marble hall here. In the
summer months there are *son et lumière* performances in the
Belvedere Park illustrating the history of the building. Take a
leisurely stroll through the park, and let the harmony of this architectural *Gesamtkunstwerk* sink in. Afterwards you may feel like
visiting the impressive painting collection which is housed in the
Upper Belvedere.

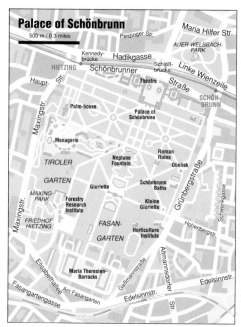

Palace of Schönbrunn

500 m / 0.3 miles

Maria Hilfer Str.

Penzinger Str.

AUER-WELSBACH-PARK

Kennedy-brücke

Hadikgasse

HIETZING

Schönbrunner

Schloß-brücke

Linke Wienzeile

Haupt-

Str.

Theatre

Straße

SCHÖN-BRUNN

Palm-house

Palace of Schönbrunn

Maxingstr.

Menagerie

Neptune Fountain

Roman Ruins

TIROLER

Obelisk

Grünbergstraße

Schwenkgasse

GARTEN

Gloriette

Schönbrunn Baths

MAXING-PARK

Forestry Research Institute

Kleine Gloriette

Maxingstr.

FRIEDHOF HIETZING

FASAN-GARTEN

Horticulture Institute

Hohenbergstr.

Gaßmannstraße

Altmannsdorfer

Str.

Maria Theresien-Barracks

Am Fasangarten

Edelsinnstr.

Elisabethallee

Edelsinnstr.

Fasangartengasse

6. The Schönbrunn

A stroll through the Schönbrunn Park surrounding the Palace; a visit to the Palace, the Gloriette, the Palm-House and the Zoo.

– U4 to Schönbrunn –

A visit to Vienna wouldn't be complete without a trip to **Schönbrunn**. Guided tours only: March, daily, 9am–4pm; April to June, and October, daily 8.30am–5pm; July to September, daily, 7.30am–5pm. The best thing is to choose a sunny day and take the U4 as far as Schönbrunn. From there you can walk along the Schlossallee – where the traffic is rather heavy – to the main gate; a nicer route, though, is to turn right at the station building and go directly into the **Schlosspark** – a magnificent park with artistically-shaped bushes and marble statues. Between April and October it's certainly worth stopping off for a coffee-break at the **Meierei** in the Kronprinzengarten. After that it's not long before you are confronted by the famous Schönbrunn-yellow facade of the 'Versailles of Austria'.

The area here used to be wooded, and it was a romantic spring that gave Schönbrunn its name (*Schöner* = beautiful, *Brunnen* = spring). It was here that Johann Bernhard Fischer von Erlach built a summer residence for the imperial family. The Palace of Schönbrunn was only completed and given its present-day magnificence under Maria Theresa, who resided here for most of her reign. Within the palace, 45 of the 1,141 rooms are open to visitors. The splendid interior decoration, mostly limited to white and gold, is internationally considered to be one of the greatest achievements of the rococo period.

In the right wing, the **Empress's Ceremonial Apartments**, including the round **Chinese Room**, may be visited. This room, formerly the Empress's study, is affectionately nicknamed the Konspirationstafelstube (conspiracy room). It was formerly used for 'secret' dinners, and to avoid untimely interruptions by servants, a fully-laid table would simply rise from the middle of the floor.

In stark contrast to all this magnificence are the almost spartan furnishings of the **State Apartments**, where Franz Joseph used to reside. He was born in Schönbrunn in 1830, and also died here (1916). In the left wing are the *salon* of Maria Theresa with its lavish wood panelling, the famous **Vieux-Lacque-Zimmer**, and the **Zeremoniensaal**. Another famous room is the **Spiegelsaal** (Hall of

Mirrors), where Mozart performed at the age of six. It was in the **Blue Chinese Drawing-Room** that Austria's last Emperor, Karl I, had to sign the paper depriving him of his right to rule, and the delegates to the Congress of Vienna once danced in the **Great Gallery**. If you are interested in old carriages you should take a look at the **Wagenburg**, which is situated a few paces beyond the south-west corner of the courtyard. There are several gorgeous coachman's liveries on display here, and around five dozen state carriages, including the *Imperialwagen*, which weighs four tons and was used at coronation ceremonies.

After this, you should go for a short walk along the wonderful *parterre* as far as the Neptune Fountain. If you carry on straight ahead you'll be able to enjoy a magnificent view from the **Gloriette**, situated on a small hill and open from May to October, daily 8am–6pm.

From the Gloriette go slightly to the left and down to the **Schönbrunner Zoo** (daily, 9am–6pm). This Baroque construction was built in 1752, and is the oldest menagerie in the world. One problem though: the demands of keeping animals properly and the facilities of old Baroque architecture don't always mix. Afterwards, you should certainly take a look at the nearby **Palmenhaus** ('Palm-House', daily, 9am–4.30pm). This pavilion-like glass and iron construction was

The Schönbrunn

built in 1880, and contains wonderful exotic plants.

And now it's time for a well-earned rest. Go straight ahead from the Palmenhaus and then to the left, and the route leads out of the Schlosspark on to the Hietzinger Platzl. From here it's only a few minutes to the venerable **Café Dommayer** (Dommayergasse 1). There's a coffee-house atmosphere here, combined with all the flair of the *belle époque*, plus a romantic summer-garden.

If you feel like eating something more substantial, though, the **Hietzinger Bräu** restaurant opposite specialises in very filling 'Old Vienna' meat dishes.

To get back to the city centre again after your meal the best thing to do is to walk back to the Hietzinger Platzl, and then along the edge of the Schlosspark until you reach the nearby U4 station of Hietzing.

7. The Prater

Walk or cycle through the district of Leopoldstadt; visit the Vienna Porcelain Manufactory in the Augarten; the Wurstlprater, the Giant Ferris Wheel and the Lilliput Railway. Take a stroll in the Prater's woods and meadows; have supper in either the Schweizerhaus or the Lusthaus.

– U4, U1 to Schwedenplatz –

Vienna's district of **Leopoldstadt** lies directly opposite the city on the other side of the Danube Canal. The island formed by the Danube and the canal provides for an interesting contrast if you don't want to limit your impressions of Vienna to the Opera House and the Hofburg. The best way of discovering Leopoldstadt and the adjoining **Prater** is by bike and these can be rented at the **Salztorbrücke**. Don't be put off by the 'mini-Manhattan' on the north bank of the canal, erected during the 1960s and 70s; beyond, in the second postal district, a piece of old Vienna remains intact.

Cross over the canal via the **Schwedenbrücke** and continue a little way along **Taborstrasse**. Until the building of the Nordbahn (northern railway) and the regulation of the Danube in 1870, this street was one of the most important in the city. Sandwiched between a row of shops, house No 10 is the old **goods exchange** which was built in 1890 and has surely seen better days. Fellini was captivated by the atmosphere of the main hall which has housed the **Serapions Theatre** for the last few years. Leopoldstadt, which was formerly the Jewish quarter of Vienna, was always home to small businessmen and craftsmen – and all those who were not welcome in the city itself, such as the butchers and tanners.

Passing the **Spital der Barmherzigen Brüder** (Hospital of the Brothers of Charity) you arrive via the Karmelitergasse on the left at the **Karmelitermarkt**. This is where the Jewish ghetto once began. The 60,000 Jews who lived here were deported and murdered during the war. Only their small shops and workshops remain, but they still exude their own special atmosphere; definitely Vienna but with a distinct southeastern European flavour. Stroll among the market stalls, between the piles of fruit and vegetables, the stands selling horsemeat and the hawkers selling clothes. Arnold Schönberg and Sigmund Freud both spent their childhood here. The area was once considered cheap and of ill-repute; today property prices are rising and Leopoldstadt is threatened with becoming chic.

Leave the city's former ghetto via the Miesbachgasse and enter the 'feudal' part of district 2, the **Augarten**. Near the entrance to the park on the right stands the **Alte Favorita**, an imperial garden palace, where the young Mozart once played the piano. Today it

Idyllic spot in the Prater

houses the **Porzellanmanufaktur Augarten**, the second oldest porcelain manufacturing centre in Europe; the palace behind it is the home of the Vienna Boys' Choir.

Going along the Heinestrasse, which was lined with huge trees in former days, we leave the Augarten and reach the circular traffic junction known as the Praterstern. From here the Lassallestrasse leads to the Reichsbrücke, to the Danube and the **Mexikoplatz** with its kitschy, pseudo-Romanesque Church of St Francis of Assisi.

The Praterstern is also where the **Praterstrasse** ends. The cycle path goes straight over the Praterstern, past Wien-Nord station and directly to the giant Ferris Wheel. Non-cyclists can take the U1 to Praterstern and continue on to the Lusthaus on a number 80A bus, or an 81A to the Freudenau horse-racing stadium.

People first started riding the 65-m (210-ft) high **Giant Ferris Wheel** in 1897. This 500-ton iron construction shares the honour with St Stephen's Cathedral of being the city's main landmark, and was also featured in the film *The Third Man*.

Around the edge of the actual Prater are the stalls of the **Wurstlprater**. One of the oldest fairgrounds in the world, the Wurstlprater has lost some of its charm through damage suffered in

Ghost train in the Prater

World War II. The magic of the past can only really be reconstructed in the nearby **Prater Museum**, with its posters and photos.

The Viennese atmosphere in the **Schweizerhaus**, on the other hand, is unrelenting. You should plan a break here: sit under the magnificent horse-chestnut trees, and indulge in the traditional feel of the place – it's at its best if you order a mug of draught Budweiser and a nice grilled *Stelze* (pickled knuckle of pork).

But if you'd rather keep such substantial delicacies for the afternoon, and first want to have a really good breakfast, then cycle the short distance to No 3, Prater Hauptallee, to the ancient **Café-Meierei-Holzdorfer**. Here you can sit on the *terrasse* surrounded by greenery. The **Prater Hauptallee**, 5km (3 miles) long, leads through magnificent woods and meadows; in 1766 Emperor Joseph II opened this former imperial game preserve to the general public.

At this point you can return to the Wurstlprater and travel 4km (2½ miles) on the **Lilliput Railway** to **Heustadlwasser**, or walk or cycle via the Hauptallee to the **Lusthaus**. This delightful Baroque pleasure pavilion was once an imperial hunting lodge and after the opening of the Prater it became a favourite meeting-place for several *Herr Barons* and their mistresses. The **Prater grove** is all around you. The only place that should perhaps be avoided in the evening is around the **Rustenschacherallee** – it's a cheap pick-up area.

8. Coffee-Houses

A brief look at a source of much local pride: the myth of the Viennese coffee-house.

Marble-top tables, a small *Brauner* (coffee with milk) and a glass of water, newspapers and *Herr Ober* (the waiter), elegant as ever with his little bow-tie, who automatically brings customers coffee the way they like it. The smell of cigarette smoke, the right atmosphere, and plenty of time – coffee-houses and stress don't go together.

'In Vienna, people go to coffee-houses to get away from it all,' wrote Heimito von Doderer, 'and everyone, an island to himself, sits as far away from everyone else as he can.' Solitude among people of like mind – it's a very Viennese way of having a good time socially, and is also just as much a feature of the 'modern' coffee-houses that have appeared in the city since the 1970s, such as the **Alt Wien**, the **Kleines Café**, the **Salzgries** or the **Engländer**. The 'island' effect is still very much there, it only appears to be somewhat more communicative.

Vienna's first ever coffee-house was

founded in the 17th century by the Armenian merchant Johannes
Diodato. The institution developed in the years that followed into
a kind of melting-pot, a meeting-place for the Vienna intelligentsia,
and finally became legendary once the *Kaffeehausliteraten* arrived
on the scene.

'A *Kaffeehausliterat* is someone in a coffee-house who has time to
reflect on things that people outside never experience,' Anton Kuh
once said about himself and his colleagues. Vienna's coffee-house
tradition is not the oldest around, but certainly the best cultivated.
It even survived the vinyl craze during the economic boom period
of the 1950s and 60s. And the restaurant and pub boom of the last
two decades has also given the coffee-house a new lease of life –
with special emphasis on those that don't look at all 'new', for a
Viennese coffee-house without any atmosphere is just as appalling a
prospect as a *Wiener Schnitzel* without any breadcrumbs.

Establishments that just managed to escape the fate of being renovated by a hair are: the 1950s-style **Prückel** on the Stubenring;
the **Sperl** in the Gumpendorfstrasse, which was opened in 1880
(once the favourite haunt of operetta kings Kalmán and Lehár);
and the **Diglas** in the Wollzeile. The modern age has also had very
little impact on the **Landtmann**, which is the oldest café on the
Ringstrasse.

One of the most attractive and also the oldest of the 500 or so
coffee-houses in Vienna is the **Frauenhuber** in the Himmelpfortgasse, which once belonged to Maria Theresa's personal chef. You
should really have breakfast here at least once during your visit to
the city: breakfast should consists of a roll and butter, a boiled egg,
a *Kipferl* (croissant) and a *melange* (coffee with milk). Another establishment with a genuinely old coffee-house atmosphere is the
Eiles on Josefstädterstrasse.

The **Central** was once the bastion of the city's *Kaffeehausliteraten*. This 'extended drawing-room' in the Palais Ferstel, formerly
filled with poets and philosophers, opened its doors again in 1986
for the first time in decades – it's an elegant but, sadly, rather soul-
less coffee-house these days. This place, which provided 'refuge for
people forced to kill time so as to avoid time killing them' (Alfred

Where's the Heuriger?

Polgar), was frequented at different times by Leon Trotsky, Anton Kuh, Egon Friedell and Peter Altenberg.

The **Griensteidl** on Michaelerplatz, which housed Vienna's *Kaffeehausliteraten* until 1897, was resurrected in 1990 – shiny and bereft of atmosphere, but despite that still the only coffee-house in all Vienna that a bank had to make way for. Sigmund Freud used to play cards here, and Arthur Schnitzler introduced the young Hoffmansthal to the place. When the Griensteidl was pulled down, Karl Kraus declared: 'The demolition people are turning Vienna into a proper metropolis now'. The interior of the café **Museum** (Friedrichstrasse 6), designed by Adolf Loos in 1899, was also demolished. But this meeting-place for the art world has retained its flair. Today's artists sit here at tables once occupied by Robert Musil, Elias Canetti and Oskar Kokoschka.

In the 1950s, doyen of literature Hans Weigel and H C Hartmann's Vienna Group turned the tiny **Hawelka** (Dorotheengasse 12) into the meeting-place for avant-garde artists. Wilhelm Holzbauer and Friedrich Torberg used to sit here, as did Oscar Werner, Ingeborg Bachmann, Henry Miller and Helmut Qualtinger. Frau Hawelka still serves the guests her legendary mini-*Buchteln* (a kind of scone), while her husband Leopold, in his waistcoat and bow-tie, pours out black coffees and glasses of *Birne* (pear schnapps). These days the artists here also include several people who come along just to be seen. But the most important things are still in place: the atmosphere, and Frau Hawelka's scones. Kurt Moldovan's famous line still applies: Es wird Zeit serviert ('Time is served').

Dummy of Peter Altenberg at one of the tables in the Central

'Heuriger' or new wine is as much a part of Vienna as the waltz or the Big Wheel.

Heuriger is the name given to the new wine (*heuer* = this year) which is usually the product of several types of grape, and is also the name given to the tavern that serves it. The most traditional type of *Heuriger* is the so-called *Buschenschank*, a very simple, rustic tavern either right next to or bang in the middle of a vineyard. A bush hung out above the entrance is a sign meaning *'ausg'steckt is'* ie the tavern is open and new wine is available. The custom dates back to the year 1784 when Emperor Joseph II allowed Vienna's winemakers to serve their own produce. The Viennese were delighted and used to travel in hordes every Sunday to what used to be the suburbs in order to sit at simple wooden tables under old horse-chestnut trees, and sample the new wine accompanied by *Schmalzbrot* (bread and dripping). This highly pleasant Sunday outing quickly developed into an institution.

Most of the old rustic taverns have now developed into fullblown *Heurigenrestaurants*, though the ones that still serve their own wine can be identified by the magic word *Eigenbau*. The larger establishments have to buy extra wine (their own alone would never suffice) and the sideboards bend under the weight of such substantial delicacies as *Backhendl* (deep fried chicken) and *Schinkenfleckerl* (noodles with diced ham). The famous *Heurigen* village of **Grinzing**, with its Schönbrunn-yellow houses, is almost suffocated these days beneath merry hordes of trippers. The legendary Viennese *Weinseligkeit* (literally: 'state of tipsiness induced by wine') is relatively hard to experience here, but if you would still like to get to know Grinzing, go to **Feuerwehr-Wagner** with its magnificent arcaded courtyard (Grinzingerstrasse 53) or to the **Oppolzer**, a higher-class *Heuriger* at Himmelstrasse 22, with the most romantic courtyard in the area and a fine buffet, with prices to match.

Ever since the Roman emperor Probus had vineyards planted here, Vienna has probably been the only metropolis in the world to have its own wine. From Bisamberg, north of the Danube, to the slopes of the Kahlenberg, from Mauer in the south to Ober-St-Veit in the west, somewhere in the region of 25,000 hectolitres (660,000 gallons) of wine are produced annually on approximately 700ha (1,730 acres) of land. The former suburbs of Nussdorf, Kahlenberger Dorf, Grinzing, Sievering, Neustift, Stammersdorf and all the rest also play their part in the statistics: the average *per capita* wine consumption here is 35 litres (9 gallons) a year.

Most of the Viennese have their 'own' secret little *Heurigen* where they can indulge in their love of *Weinseligkeit* and *Gemütlichkeit* to the full – the **Baumeister Friedreich** in Ottakring, for example (20 Liebhartstalstrasse), where you sit on the steep slope of the Wilhelminenberg surrounded by vineyards, and can leave the noisy bustle of the city far behind. On the western edge of the city, in Nussdorf or in Kahlenbergerdorf, the atmosphere is almost completely rural – at the **Schübl-Auer** (Kahlenbergstrasse 22) you sit in a courtyard filled with nut trees and horse-chestnuts.

There's a highly traditional time to be had north of the Danube, too, in **Stammersdorf**; you can get there very easily on a No 31 tram (from Schottenring/U2). Along the very rural-looking high street you'll find one *Heurigen* after another – with leafy courtyards and simple wooden benches. A large information board at the tram stop will tell you which places have *'ausg'steckt'* (ie opened their young wine). First though, wander through the picturesque alleyways at the foot of the Bisamberg, past the winepresses and cellars, some of which are as much as 300 years old.

Music, of course, is an integral part of the *Heurigen* myth. *Schrammelmusik*, named after the Schrammel brothers, soon conquered the hearts of the Viennese. *Heurigen* songs are all about wine, life, death and the transience of things. Most of them are sad, but once you've reached that special state of *Weinseligkeit*, sadness and happiness tend to merge together. 'Es wird a Wein sein, und wir wer'n nimmer sein' ('Wine'll still be around when we're dead').

10. On the Blue Danube

A few minutes from the city centre by U-Bahn you can find surfing, sailing and sun-bathing. The following tours can be undertaken on a bicycle or are accessible through public transport.

– U1, Kagran –

Donauinsel

Hire a bicycle at the Danube Canal near Salztorbrücke and follow the signposted bicycle path to the **Reichsbrücke**, from where you can drive onto the 21-km (13-mile) long artificial island (the Donauinsel), which was built in 1981. There is a station near the bridge (U1-Donauinsel).

The **Donauinsel** is a by-product of the construction of the New Danube canal, which was equipped with sluice gates and designed to counter flooding.

A 200-metre (600-ft) wide strip
of land between the new canal
and the old river, the island
has since become a recre-
ational resort with Austria's
longest beach (40 km/24
miles) and mile-long paths for pedestri-
ans and bicycles. It is a 'green lung', only a few minutes
from the city centre, where you can jog, cycle, dive, surf, sail,
swim, row or skateboard.

Holiday resort atmosphere à la Torremolinos begins right at the
Reichsbrücke at the **Copa Kagrana**. Here, about 40 bars and
restaurants – Turkish, Greek, Italian – try to create a seaside holiday atmosphere in the heart of Vienna. Open-air discos thrive at
night. The **Donauinselfest** has been held here every June since
1984; it's a spectacular festival with concerts, cabaret and theatre
performances.

North of the Copa is the **Aquadrom**, Austria's longest water
chute, and next to it the **Aquadrom Beach Club** with its disco and
spare-ribs from the barbecue. The northern part of the island is
usually less busy. You can swim in small, sandy bays while enjoying
the view of the hills of the Vienna Woods. Sailors find the best con-
ditions for their sport in this part of the island.

Trams 31 and 32 will drop you directly at the northern end of
the island. In the southern half of the island, opposite the left bank
of the New Danube canal between Wehr (weir) 2 and Lobgrund-
strasse, nudists will find their own paradise. And if you enjoy din-
ing *al fresco*, then book one of the many barbecue areas (Tel: 4000,
direct line 82 677).

The Old Danube

If you continue along the bicycle path from the Reichsbrücke, you
get to the **Old Danube**, a former branch of the Danube river. Here
you'll find unofficial spots to swim as well as public bathing places
such as the **Gänsehäufl** (which literally and unfortunately translates
as 'goose droppings') and can also be reached by underground (U1
to Kagran) or by bus (91A to the terminus). A foot-bridge crosses
over to the island. The Gänsehäufl was once Europe's oldest public
baths, dating back to the turn of the century.

Further north are the **Strandbad Alte Donau** and the **Arbeiter-
strandbad** (workers' baths). Both can be reached on the U1 (Alte
Donau). From there you have to take the bus (20B) or walk along
An der Oberen Alten Donau. Here there are further opportunities
for recreation, be they lying on the river bank, hiring a boat for
sailing, or paddling a pedalo.

Many bars and restaurants with beautiful gardens cater for visitors to this area. Try **Birners Strandgasthaus** (An der Oberen Alten Donau 47) or alternatively the **Neubrasilien** (An der Unteren
Alten Donau 61).

A selection of the best collections.

– U2/U3 to Volkstheater –

It would be a shame to visit Vienna without looking at its museums. The **Kunsthistorisches Museum** (Museum of Fine Arts, Maria Theresienplatz) for example: this magnificent domed building is one of the five most important art museums in the world, and contains masterpieces by Breughel, Tintoretto, Titian and Rubens.

The **Naturhistorisches Museum** (Museum of Natural History) is in the twin building opposite. Exhibits include the oldest collection of meteorites in the world, a precious stone collection with the largest opal found in Europe and a palaeontological collection.

Vienna also boasts the largest collection of graphic art in the world. The **Albertina** (Augustinerstrasse 1), contains 1.9 million examples of printed graphic art and drawings spanning five centuries – from Michelangelo and Dürer to Raphael, Rembrandt and Picasso. Anyone interested in 19th- and 20th-century art will find a remarkable collection of masterpieces by Klimt and Schiele, Kokoschka, Boeckl and Wotruba in the **Österreichische Galerie** (Austrian Gallery) in the Upper Belvedere.

A few minutes away from the Belvedere is the **Museum des 20. Jahrhunderts** (Museum of the 20th Century). The former Austria pavilion of the Brussels World Fair of 1958 features various exhibitions taken from the **Museum Moderner Kunst** (Museum of Modern Art), which has been in the Palais Liechtenstein since 1979.

Vienna's **Museum für Angewandte Kunst (MAK)** (Museum of Applied and Decorative Art, Stubenring 5) is the oldest of its kind in Europe. The exhibits include furniture, carpets, porcelain and textiles from the Middle Ages to the present day. At the Hofburg was the **Schatzkammer** (Imperial Treasury, with the 1,000-year-old Imperial Crown) but a fire has temporarily closed it.

The **Historisches Museum** (Historical Museum, Karlsplatz) documents Vienna's history from the Stone Age to the present day; highlights here include scale models of the city's development, stained glass from the Cathedral and Adolf Loos' drawing-room.

For everyone who has been trying for years to gain access to the Friedensreich Hundertwasser house, the highly colourful public housing complex in Kegelgasse, a Hundertwasser museum has been set up on the initiative of some of the city's painters and PR people: the **KunstHaus Wien**, which was opened in 1991.

Vienna also has a great many smaller museums – the **Theatermuseum** (Theatre Museum) in the Lobkowitz palace, the **Uhrenmuseum** (Horological Museum, Schulhof 2), the **Sigmund Freud Museum**, situated in Freud's former home at Berggasse 19, the **Beethoven Museum** (Probusgasse 6), the **Mozart Museum** (Figarohaus, Domgasse 5) and the **Haydn Museum** (Haydngasse 19), to name but a few.

12. Splendid Cemeteries

A walk through some of Vienna's finest burial grounds.

–Tram No 71, from Schwarzenbergplatz –

The relationship of the Viennese to death is legendary. They spend their lives saving money at a *Sterbeverein* (rough translation: 'death club') in order to be considered a *'schöne Leich'* ('a nice corpse') and to be given an elegant *Pompfüneberer* ('funeral') to the sound of wailing violins. Most Viennese songs are preoccupied with death, too, a mixture of acceptance of fate and a strong yearning – *'Verkauft's mei G'wand, i fahr in Himmel'* ('I'm off to Heaven – sell my clothes').

At the beginning of November (All Saints' Day) each year the city's tram system provides 500 extra carriages on route 71 to convey nearly a million people to the **Zentralfriedhof** (central cemetery) in Simmering, which lies along the length of Vienna's longest street, the Simmeringer Hauptstrasse. Before the airport *autobahn* was built, the first sight most visitors had of Vienna on arrival was the infinitely long wall of this cemetery, the largest in Austria, whose 2 million graves outnumber the actual population of the city itself.

The Zentralfriedhof

Get off your 71 tram at Friedhofstor 1. Behind it is the **Jewish Cemetery** – an overgrown wilderness, with a few of the tombstones still lying on the ground. Many relatives of the dead who lie here were deported and murdered. The graves are divided into groups, and in group 5b Arthur Schnitzler, Friedrich Torberg and Karl Kraus lie buried. Also here is the grave of Gustav Pick, long-forgotten composer of the famous *Fiaker Song*. Along the cemetery wall, the way leads to the main gate, **Tor (Gate) 2**. It was built by Max Hegele, who in 1905 also constructed the imposing-looking **Dr. Karl-Lueger-Remembrance Church**, a short distance to the left of the main gate. This church, with its huge dome, is considered a *Jugendstil* masterpiece. Instead of numerals, the clock-face spells out the letters *Tempus Fugit* (Time Flies).

To the right and left of the main path is probably the largest collection of 'tombs of honour' in the world. Approximately 1,000 personalities lie buried in this cemetery, which was opened in 1874. Every day, huddles of camera-clicking Japanese stand in front of the graves of Beethoven, Brahms, Gustav Mahler and Schubert.

The silhouette of a bat can be made out on the gravestone of waltz king Johann Strauss the Younger, a tribute to what is probably his most famous opera, *die Fledermaus*; the grave of Helmut Qualtinger is adorned with a sculpture by Alfred Hrdlicka, and actor Curt Jürgens was the first to receive a nocturnal burial at his own request. His gravestone is jet black marble. Mozart has been given a monument in group 32a, but he actually died a pauper, whose coffin was blessed in an anonymous ceremony for that day's dead.

The cemetery, with its 15,000 trees, is one of the largest expanses of green in the city, and its surface area – 2.4km^2 (1 square mile) – is nearly as large as Vienna's District 1. It even has its own hunting association to take care of the many rabbits, pheasants and partridges. The 300,000 graves also provide a cross-section of Viennese history – there are splendid vaults, paupers' graves, and the names of Italian, Serbian and Hungarian noblemen and captains in the imperial cavalry. The cemetery has its own bus, which travels across it, and a plan containing the grave numbers is available from the supervisor at the main gate.

Around All Saints' Day, flower sellers, sausage stallholders and *Maronibrater* (hot chestnut vendors) all pitch their tents here. Opposite the main gate is the majestic-looking **crematorium**, built by Clemens Holzmeister in 1922. This Byzantine-Expressionist building is enclosed in the walls of the Renaissance palace of **Neugebäude**, a summer residence of the emperor Maximilian dating from the 16th century. The building became dilapidated soon after its completion. A substantial amount of its splendid facade decoration was used in the construction of the Gloriette at Schönbrunn. During the Turkish siege of 1529 – which didn't succeed, but did bring coffee to Vienna – the Sultan's tent is rumoured to have stood here. If you cross the allotments, it's possible to walk along the walls of the palace's former pheasantry.

The enticing-looking **Schloss Concordia** is situated opposite gate number one of the cemetery. This romantic pavilion, restored in 1988, in the middle of its sleepy garden, is a cross between a café, a restaurant and a literary salon. The interior is crowned by a *Jugendstil* glass roof. If you have the time and the inclination for more graves, take a No 71 tram back towards the city centre a short way until you reach the magnificent **St Marx's Cemetery** at Leberstrasse 6. It has been deconsecrated for over 100 years and is Vienna's last *Biedermeier* cemetery. Today it is a romantic park, filled with the heady scent of lilac blossom in the springtime. It was here in 1791 that Mozart was buried, in an unmarked grave. Walk

View of the Kahlenberg

a short way through this idyllic place, past the graves of silk-manufacturers and small-time craftsmen.

Once back in the city centre, you can discover more about the city's past at the unusual **Burial Museum** (Bestattungs-museum), probably the only one of its kind in the world, where the 600 or so exhibits include special alarm clocks to wake people who seem to be dead but aren't, funeral coaches and luxury coffins. Still on this macabre note, go on to the **Josephinum**, founded in 1785 by Joseph II as a Military Academy of Surgery and Medicine.

13. Tales from the Vienna Woods

Three walks through the 'green lungs' of the city.

When the people of Vienna feel like a walk in the woods, they don't have far to travel. The **Vienna Woods** *(Wienerwald)*, those 50-km (30 mile) long north-eastern foothills of the Alps, extend right into the city itself.

In the Danube area they drop steeply and surround part of the city rather like an amphitheatre. Dense mixed forest, gentle hills and slopes with vineyards and small *Heurigendörfer* (wine-producing villages) are inviting destinations. In the summertime the ground underfoot is covered with thick moss, in spring the air is full of the scent of wild garlic, and in the autumn the colourful leaves rustle beneath your feet. It is a magnificent recreation area, with its slender elms, majestic beech trees and mighty oaks, though they are all suffering from the effects of pollution. Proximity to the city also has its disadvantages: 60 per cent of the trees here are already affected.

You can go by car on your outing to the Vienna Woods, or by public transport – or, in some cases, on foot if you prefer. Avoid weekends if at all possible, because that's when the marked routes and restaurants are all filled with masses of oxygen-starved Viennese on day-trips.

Kahlenberg and Leopoldsberg

The best thing to do is to take the U4 as far as **Heiligenstadt** and then bus number 38A. It takes you up to the Cobenzl, the Leopoldsberg and the Kahlenberg via the wine village of Grinzing and the **Höhenstrasse**. If travelling by car you can drive the entire length of the Höhenstrasse as far as Hütteldorf, or you can branch off at Kahlenberg and go to Klosterneuburg.

If you're only interested in a short outing, get off the bus at

Cobenzl and enjoy the fine view of the city from the terrace of the Cobenzl Café. The next thing to do is to find out a little bit about the various footpaths in the region. You can then walk along the narrow Reisenbergweg past some vineyards and down to **Grinzing**, where you can catch the bus again. Or you can walk a little further along the Höhenstrasse from Cobenzl, and then turn left down Himmelstrasse. If you now follow the sign saying *zur Bellevuestrasse* you'll soon come across a small monument. This is the former site of the 'Belle Vue' villa, where Sigmund Freud often spent his summers.

Take the Himmelstrasse back again, where at No 22 the Oppolzer – one of Vienna's most romantic (and expensive) *Heuriger* – awaits you. Afterwards you can take a nice walk through the **Gspöttgraben** to the neighbouring village of **Sievering**. There are some wonderful *Heurigengärten* here, too. Bus No 39A will take you back to the U-Bahn at Heiligenstadt.

You can travel on from Cobenzl with a No 38A as well, and discover the **Kahlenberg** and the **Leopoldsberg** hills. The **Festungsturm** (fortified tower) of the fortress once built by the Babenbergs up on the Leopoldsberg affords a magnificent view of the Danube and the city. The **Sobieski Chapel** is a reminder of the time when the King of Poland rushed to the assistance of the Viennese when they were fighting off the Turks. Both mountains have restaurants to greet the weary wanderer. Here you can put your feet up, have something to eat and, above all, enjoy the superb view.

Up the Hermannskogel

A trip to the legendary mountain known as the **Hermannskogel** is also worthwhile and not too strenuous either. From Heiligenstadt (U4) you should take a 39A bus all the way to its terminus in **Sievering**. Here you should go uphill along the Agnesgasse and then turn right on to the Salmannsdorfer Höhe when you reach the wayside shrine.

Go under the Höhenstrasse and then turn left, following the red markers, until you reach the 454-metre (1,480-ft) high **Dreimarkstein** mountain with its fine view. You can go into the little **Häuserl am Roan** restaurant, then go back downhill to the right, following the blue markers this time, which take you past the **Grüaß-di-a-Gott** restaurant on the Rohrerweise to Hermannskogelweg. If you now follow the green markers you'll soon reach the top of the **Hermannskogel**. From the Habsburgwarte observation point, built in 1888, you'll be greeted by a magnificent view; visibility here on clear days is over 180km (110 miles), all the way to the Traunstein in the west.

Calendar of Special Events

month ie 11 November, but on that day in Vienna you'll be more likely to be invited to a *Martinsgansl-Essen*, where people dine on roast goose in honour of St Martin. The season of the great balls and *Gschnase* (fancy dress balls) only begins in earnest once the New Year has started. The ball starts rolling, so to speak, with the – unfortunately rather touristy – *Kaiserball* (Imperial Ball) in the Hofburg, and the real highlight is the dazzling *Opernball* (Opera Ball), attended by the Austrian President, on the last Thursday of the Carnival season. Almost every professional association and club holds its own special ball: police inspectors, café-owners, chimney-sweeps, hunters (wearing the traditional green) and also doctors, lawyers, pharmacists and the fire brigade. At the *Zuckerbäckerball* a Ball Queen is selected, and her weight in sweets is then usually donated to children's villages.

Debutants and debutantes alike throng to the Opernball and the Philharmonikerball as well as to Rudolfina Redoute in order to dance the opening polonaise. The official *Ballkalender* (Ball Calendar) appears in the late autumn and may also be

JANUARY/FEBRUARY

New Year's Eve (Silvester) The Viennese assemble on the Stephansplatz to see in the New Year when the big bell called the *Pummerin* strikes 12; in the Musikverein the Vienna Philharmonic perform their New Year's Concert (*Silvesterkonzert*) which is broadcast worldwide; the Imperial Ball (*Kaiserball*) is held in the Hofburg.

Fasching (Carnival) and Ball season *Fasching*, or Carnival, officially begins on the 11th day of the 11th

obtained from the Stadtinformation (Information office) at the Town Hall, Friedrich-Schmidt-Platz 1, 1082 Wien.

Ash Wednesday (Aschermittwoch) At the end of Carnival, most restaurants and hotels 'sweeten' the transition to the dreariness of Lent with a huge *Heringschmaus* (literally: herring banquet).

Dance Festival (Tanz-Wochen) Every two years (even years: 1992, 1994, 1996 etc), in February/March, Vienna hosts a large Dance Festival.

MARCH/APRIL

Vienna Spring Fair (Wiener Frühjahrsmesse) In March, the traditional Vienna Spring Fair is held on the exhibition site in the Prater.

Easter Markets (Ostermärkte)
The *Hernalser Kalvarienbergmarkt* (March), 1170, Kalvarienberggasse.
The Easter market on the Spittelberg (weekend before Easter).

Fashion Fair (Modemesse) In April and October the avant-garde fashion fair Off-Line moves into the Hofburg.

Spring Marathon (Frühlingsmarathon) At the end of April, Vienna greets the spring with a large-scale city marathon.

City Festival (Stadtfest) On the last Saturday in April, the traditional City Festival sponsored by the ÖVP (the Austrian Conservative party) livens up Vienna's streets and squares with performances of music, cabaret and theatre.

MAY/JUNE

Danube Island Festival (Donauinselfest) This is the SPÖ's (Social Democrats) answer to the above festival; it takes place on the Donauinsel between May and June.

Vienna Festival (Wiener Festwochen) In May and June this cultural festival, both traditional and avant-garde, takes place all over Vienna.

JULY/AUGUST

Vienna Musical Summer (Wiener Musiksommer) A very broad-ranging programme of musical performances held in such attractive venues as the Staatsoper, the Arkadenhof in the Town Hall, churches and old palaces.

SEPTEMBER/OCTOBER

Vienna Autumn Fair (Wiener Herbstmesse) The Vienna Autumn Fair begins the post-summer season in September.

National Holiday (Nationalfeiertag), 26 October Recently declared National Hiking Day. A useful tip for all art fans: entry to Vienna's museums is free on this day.

Modern Vienna (Wien Modern) Claudio Abbado's festival of 20th-century music is held between the end of October and December.

DECEMBER

Christmas Markets (Christkindlmärkte) Christmas markets take place on December weekends on the Spittelberg and on the Freyung. There's an art market in the Heiligenkreuzerhof, and the square in front of the Town Hall is where the Vienna Christmas market *(Wiener Christkindlmarkt)* sets up its stalls (see also 'Markets' in the *Shopping* chapter).

More information about events can be obtained from Vienna Tourist Information (Kärntnerstrasse 38), from Stadtinformation (Town Hall, Friedrich-Schmidt-Platz 1, 1082 Wien, Tel: 4038989) and also in the *Falter*, the weekly *What's On* guide.

Shopping

The following tips are a subjective selection of old friends and new discoveries, and all of them should give you several ideas – depending on your mood and the state of your wallet – of how to part with your *schillings* in Vienna.

Books and Magazines

Whether it's a travel guide you're after, a map or a hiking guide – **Freytag & Berndt** (Kohlmarkt 9) will almost certainly stock it. The **Morawa** bookshop (Wollzeile 11) is well laid-out and stocks domestic and international newspapers. International books and magazines on art and architecture can all be found at the **Prachner** bookshop (Kärntnerstrasse 30) and the **Wolfrum** (Augustinerstrasse 10); those looking for very large and very expensive art books will appreciate the **Sallmayer'sche Buchhandlung** (Neuer Markt 6). The **Gerold** bookstore (Graben 31) and **Frick** (Graben 27) offer a wide selection of national and international books, as does the **Internationale Buchhandlung** in the Trattnerhof. Books and magazines in English can be found at **Shakespeare & Company** (Sterngasse 2) and in the **British Book Shop** (Weihburggasse 8); French books are at **Kosmos** (1090, Berggasse 12 and Wollzeile 16). Feminist literature and social science publications are all at **Brigitte Hermann** (Grünangergasse 1) as well as at the **Frauenbuchhandlung** (1080, Langegasse 11). Anyone interested in political science should drop in at **Heinz Kolisch** (Grillparzerstrasse 7). Esoteric books are at **777** (Domgasse 8) and **Südwind** (Kleeblattgasse 4); the best though is **Stonehenge** (1030, Löwengasse 31). **WfB Taschenbuchladen** (Singerstrasse 7) specialises in paperbacks. A real treasure trove is **Hintermayer** (1070, Neubaugasse 27) which sells remainders at unbelievably low prices.

Most kiosks in the city centre are open seven days a week and usually have international as well as domestic newspapers and magazines.

Austriana and Antiques

Few cities have as many antique shops in such a small area as Vienna; they are all clustered round the **Dorotheum**. *Tante Dorothee* or *Pfandl* are just two nicknames for this institution, the largest auction house in Europe. It was founded as a pawnbroker's in 1788. For 200 years now the Dorotheum has been located in a former monastery in the Dorotheergasse; today it is a cross between Old Vienna tradition, a modern auction house and a pawnbroker's (Dorotheergasse 11 and 17).

The largest selection of imperial Austrian knick-knacks is found at **k.u.k. Kuriositäten** *(*Himmelpfortgasse 9). **Duschek & Scheed** (Plankengasse 6) specialise in old watches; paintings and *objets d'art* can be found at **Reinhold Hofstätter** (Bräunerstrasse 12), *Jugendstil* objects at **Zettar** (Lobkowitzplatz 1), antique glass at **Kovacek** (Stallburggasse 2), wonderful furniture and glass at **Monika Kaesser** (Krugerstrasse 17), and antique sheet music at **Doblinger** (Dorotheergasse 10).

Markets

Halfway between the (expensive) antiques on offer from professional dealers on the one hand and cheap junk on the other, you just might (if you have patience as well as luck) find the odd fine piece at the Vienna flea market, or **Flohmarkt**, too (every Saturday until 2pm; U4/Kettenbrückengasse). Anyone who likes strolling around market stalls should also visit the **Naschmarkt**, Vienna's largest daily market, between the Karlsplatz and Kettenbrückengasse.

From May until September the **Kunst und Antiquitätenmarkt** (Arts and Antiques market) is held at the Donaukanal (Saturday 2–8pm, Sunday 10am–8pm; U2/Schottenring).

On the Spittelberg in district 7, a **Kunsthandwerksmarkt** (Arts and Crafts Fair) is held on the first weekend of every month (U2, U3 Volkstheater); in the Heiligerkreuzerhof a **Kunstmarkt** (Art Market) is held on the first weekend in every month.

Arts, Crafts and Textiles

Whether it's English velvet, French silk or material with *Wiener Werkstätte* (Vienna workshops) designs all over it – **Backhausen** (Kärntnerstrasse/Johannesgasse) stocks absolutely everything.

Magnificently colourful materials can also be obtained from **India** (Strobelgasse 2). Arts and crafts from *Österreichische Werkstätte* can be found at Kärntnerstrasse 6, and quite a few charming and original pieces can be found at the Arts and Crafts Fair at the **Spittelberg** (see under Markets).

Prints, Posters and Postcards
The best place for elegant prints by old and new masters is **Wofrum** at Augustinerstrasse 10; the **Galerie Image** (Rupprechtsplatz 4–5) has a very large selection of posters with frames and also some very fine postcards; original postcards can also be obtained at the **Karteninsel** (1040, Naschmarkt, Stand 333).

Records, Tapes and CDs
Columbia (Kärntnerstrasse 30) has a good selection, as does **Carola** (Albertina-Passage) and **Dome** (Haas-Haus on the Stephansplatz, 3rd floor) which specialises in classical music. A large selection of pop, jazz, rock and oldies are on offer at **Meky** (Operngasse 14 and Morzinplatz/Salzgries); jazz fans should take a look at **Red Octopus** (1080, Josefstädterstrasse 99); and it's hard to leave the CD shop **Gellesz** (1070, Neubaugasse 53) without a couple of new discs under your arm.

Glass, Porcelain and Tableware
Anyone keen on elegant tableware will enjoy **Lobmeyr** (Kärntnerstrasse 26); glass design ranges from Josef Hoffmann to Matteo Thun. If you're keen to buy, make sure you take a look over the road at **Wahliss** (Kärntnerstrasse 13–15) as well.

The products of the former imperial porcelain manufacturers **Augarten** can be found at the corner of Graben and Seilergasse, and a few doors further on it's worth dropping into **Rasper** (corner of Graben and Habsburgergasse). People after unusually designed tableware should visit **Ostovits** (Stephansplatz/Jasomirgottstrasse). For elegant knives and forks, **Berndorf** (Wollzeile 12) is good, as are **Besteck-Kistl** (Lichtensteg/Bauernmarkt), **WMF** (Stock-im-Eisen-Platz 3) or the very exclusive **Christofle** (Kohlmarkt 18).

Jewellery
Graben and the Kohlmarkt are where the city's long-established jewellery firms are based, some of which still proudly use the old imperial prefix *k.u.k. Hoflieferant*. **Rozet & Fischmeister** (Kohlmarkt 11) do fine silver jewellery, as do **Kiss & Rozsa** (Kohlmarkt 16) a few steps further on; **Schullin** (Kohlmarkt 7) not only has exclusive

jewellery, it also has a magnificent portal by top architect Hans Hollein. In the Graben we have **Haban** (Graben 12 and Kärntnerstrasse 2) and **Heldwein** (Graben 13). Particularly fine silver jewellery can be seen at **Kecksilber** (Trattnerhof and Bäckerstrasse 10). **Galerie V&V** (Bauernmarkt 19) specialises in modern designer jewellery from Austria and abroad, and **Schmollgruber** can be found in the smallest house in Vienna (district 7, Burggasse 3).

Knick-knacks, Presents & Souvenirs

Karfunkel (Franz-Josephs-Kai 31) sells wacky presents and fashion jewellery; **Paperbox** (Stephansplatz 6 and Graben 29A) does small presents and souvenirs; **Gimmick's** (1070, Neubaugasse 15) does totally insane presents. Gifts and crazy stationery can be found at **Angerer & Göschl** (Kleeblattgasse 4); **Eva Eder** (1080, Langegasse 19) does nice things with glass. There's a large selection of candles at the shop designed by Hans Hollein called **Retti** (Kohlmarkt 10); all kinds of Vienna souvenirs are provided by **Geschenkg'wölb** (Fleischmarkt 16) and by **Hannerl** (Jasomirgottstrasse 4). Exclusive stuff – from champagne salvers to porcelain figures – can be found at **Förster** (Kohlmarkt 5). **Haas & Haas** (Stephansplatz 4), too, is one of the best addresses for tea, presents and souvenirs.

Spectacles

Most of the international names in designer spectacles are manufactured in Austria. Try **Hartmann** (Singerstrasse 8/entry to Liliengasse); **Schau Schau** (Rotenturmstrasse 11/Ertlgasse); and **Optiker Maurer** (1080, Josefstädterstrasse/Buchfeldgasse).

Design and Furniture

Italian and Scandinavian furniture and beautiful items of designer furniture can be found at **Wolfgang Bischof** (Judenplatz 6) and at **Passini** (Franziskanerplatz 6), at **Henn** (Naglergasse 29), at **Silenzio** (Salztorgasse 3), at **Prodomo** (1150, Flachgasse 35), at **Kommode** (1080, Lerchenfelderstrasse 12), at **Officina** (Krugerstrasse 18) and also at **Accento Nuovo** (1090, Kinderspitalgasse 1). Aficionados can find furniture by Josef Hoffmann, Otto Wagner, Kolo Moser, etc for a small fortune at the **Galerie Ambiente** (Lugeck 1) and also at **Monika Kaesser** (Krugerstrasse 17); furniture by the Thonet brothers and a lot of other furniture can be found at Kohlmarkt 6. Anyone looking for a *Jugendstil* piece should take a walk down the Siebensterngasse behind the Spittelberg in district 7. Fans of the post-modern era should drop in at the **20th century** gallery at Bauernmarkt 9.

Shoes for sale

Linen & Lingerie

The **Schwäbische Jungfrau** (Graben 26) does very fine tablecloths and bed-linen, as does **Gans** (Brandstätte 1). Silk lingerie can be found at **Rosita** (Kärntnerstrasse 17); it's also worth visiting **La Biancheria** (1080, Josefstädterstrasse 27), **Per la Donna** (Fütterergasse 1) and **Mata** (1070, Lerchenfeldstrasse 31).

Shoes & Leather Goods

People looking for something special go to Italian establishments such as **Tardi's** (Kärntnerstrasse 37, Bauernmarkt 2 and Graben 17), **d'Ambrosio** (Jasomirgottstrasse 4–6 and Bauernmarkt), **Magli** (Stephansplatz 2) and **Dominici** (Singerstrasse 2), or they go for eccentric French chic at **Kélian** (Bauernmarkt 12). Made-to-measure shoes are manufactured by **Rudulf Scheer** (Bräunerstrasse 4).

As far as leather is concerned, **Bottega Veneta** is excellent but unbelievably expensive (Stock-im-Eisen-Platz 3/entrance to Seilergasse); belts in all colours and styles are the speciality of **Vogue** (Tuchlauben 12); highly exclusive leather goods can be purchased at **Louis Vuitton** (Kohlmarkt 16); and high-quality hand-made goods can be found at **Franz Schulz** (Führichgasse 6). The **Kofferzentrale** (1060, Mariahilferstrasse 3) does suitcases and handbags in every conceivable shape, size and colour.

Elegant Fashion & Haute Couture

British chic and modern fashion is at **Kowalski**, **Piccina** and **Mac's** in the Brandstätte; international names in haute couture can be found at **Jonak** (Trattnerhof), **Trussardi** (Tuchlauben 11 and the Haas-Haus on the Stephansplatz), **Jil Sander** (Bauernmarkt) and **Sonia Rykiel** (Goldschmiedgasse 5). **Etoile** (Lugeck/Köllnerhofgasse) and **Cellini** (Jasomirgottstrasse 5) both do clothing by Armani, Krizia and Valentino. Conservative British style is worshipped at **Ita** and **Braun** at Graben 8 and 18 respectively. **Popp & Kretschmer** (Kärntnerstrasse/Walfischgasse) and **Adlmüller** (Kärntnerstrasse 41) sell super-elegant dresses.

Men's Fashion

The men's fashion specialists in Vienna are **Willi Silbernagl** (Kärntnerstrasse 13–15), **Pal Zileri** (Jasòmirgottstrasse 4) and **Sir Anthony** (Kärntnerstrasse 21); **fil à fil** (Brandstätte 7–9) has a huge assortment of men's shirts; tailor-made clothing can be obtained from the best tailor in the city, **Knize** (Graben 13).

Young People's Fashion

The creations of Helmut Lang, an Austrian fashion designer who has had a lot of success in Paris, can be found at Bauernmarkt 2a;

young fashion trio **Schella Kann** come across as classical-refined (Singerstrasse 6/2/8 and Seilergasse 3); **Assasyn** (Sterngasse 2) does weird things to traditional dress; Austrian knitted designs, classical and original, are all at **Haider-Petkov** (Kohlmarkt 11); and **Annette Beaufays** (Bäckerstrasse 10) does young avant-garde stuff.

Classical-refined fashion is also at **Cachil** (Marc-Aurel-Strasse/Vorlaufstrasse) and at **Giarratana** on the Lugeck; relaxed young elegance is at **Neumann** (Seilergasse 3), and the British touch is in evidence at **Kowalski** (Brandstätte 7–9); rather more 'sophisticated' shops include **Kali** (Bauernmarkt 12), **Skaf** (Jasomirgottstrasse 12) and **Firis** (Ruprechtsplatz/Sterngasse); those keen on loose, casual clothing go to **Mac's** (Brandstätte 7–9), to **Stefanel** (Haas-Haus on the Stephansplatz), to **Fortuna** (Tuchlauben 12) or to **Blaumax** (Fleischmarkt 20). Weirder stuff, jeans and American jackets can be found along Judengasse: at **Topper** and **Tomaso**, **Judengasse 3**, and at **Frontline** and **Sabotage**.

Department Stores & Shopping Centres

Vienna's traditional department stores **Herzmansky** and **Gerngross** are on Mariahilferstrasse (26–30 as well as the entrance to Kirchengasse 6); a few metres further on, at the corner of Amerlingstrasse, stands the **Generali-Center**, renovated in 1990. That same year the **Galleria** on the Landstrasser Haupstrasse in district 3 was also added, the **Haas-Haus** on the Stephansplatz, with its exclusive shops, was opened, and in district 17, close to the Gürtel, an enterprising Viennese architect built the **Lugner-City** shopping centre (1150, Gablenzgasse 5). On the other side of the Danube in the northern part of the city is the **Donauzentrum** (U1), and **Shopping City Süd** can be found in the south.

Hairdressers

Pop stars and journalists, advertising reps and junior bankers – they all go to **Erich** (Griechengasse 7). More solid local stars are the brothers **Bundy & Bundy** (Habsburgergasse 3), who have been around a long time, and the **Gruppa l'ultima** (Köllnerhofgasse 3), who are good at chic styling. For 1950s chic visit **Werner Berndorfer** (Jasomirgottstrasse 5). One very sophisticated establishment is **Ramé** (Walfischgasse 2).

Dry-Cleaning

Stross (Bauernmarkt 3) have a 24-hour dry-cleaning service.

Tea

Tea and lots of useful and beautiful extras to go with it can be had at **Schönbichler** (Wollzeile 5), which was founded in 1870, and at **Jäger** (Operngasse 6); there is also a large selection at **Haas & Haas** (Stephansplatz 4) and **Demmer's Teehaus** (Mölkerbastei 5).

Wine
Wine lovers will be enchanted as they wander through the old vault at **Grams & Co.** (Singerstrasse 26); also to be recommended are the **Vinothek St Stephan** (Stephansplatz 6), which also provides select olive oils, **Zum Finsteren Stern** (Sterngasse 6) and the **Vinothek bei der Piaristenkirche** (1080, Piaristengasse 54).

Cakes & Confectionery
The world-famous *Sachertorte* can be obtained at Philharmoniker-strasse 4, at the entrance to Kärntnerstrasse, and its 'competitors', along with very beautifully packaged confectionery, at **Demel** (Kohlmarkt 14). *Imperial-Torte* (Emperor Cake) is on sale at the Bristol and Imperial Hotels; Vienna's latest cake creation, the triangular *Domspitz*, can be enjoyed at the **Do & Co** Café on the seventh floor of the Haas-Haus on the Stephansplatz. Real cake fans will find everything they want in the long-established **Gerstner** (Kärntnerstrasse 15) and **Heiner** (Kärntnerstrasse 21 and Wollzeile 9). The **Kurkonditorei Oberlaa** (Neuer Markt 16) also has a fine range – from chocolates to *Joghurttörtchen* (yoghurt-cake).

Belgian chocolates can be enjoyed at **Godiva** (Graben 17) and at **Fabienne** (Wollzeile 5); and **Altmann & Kühne** (Graben 30) sell Viennese chocolate specialities packed in magnificent little boxes.

Gourmet Fare & Luxury Snacks
Vienna's top address for gourmets is **Meinl am Graben** (Graben 19), and hot and cold snacks are served at the rear of the store (in the **Lukullus-Bar**. Open on weekdays until 8pm is **Meinl Gourmet** on the Opernring. The delicatessens and snack-bars at the **Schwarzes Kamel** (Bognergasse 5), at **Wild** (Neuer Markt 10) and **Böhle** (Wollzeile 30) are all very traditional. Gourmet food and tasty snacks, with the emphasis on fish and seafood, can be found at **Do & Co** (Akademiestrasse 3), and excellent Italian food is offered by **Da Conte** on the Judenplatz, **Piccini** near the Naschmarkt (1060, Linke Wienzeile 4) and the tiny **Urbanek** restaurant at the Naschmarkt.

Many different and delicious types of bread can be found at the marvellous old **Grimm** bakery (Kurrentgasse 10), and also at **Elias** at Fleischmarkt 18 (the delicious *Kartoffelbrot* is a must).

Eating Out

The boom in pub custom in the early 1980s has also given the Viennese gastronomic scene a great deal more variety. The home of 'Viennese Cuisine' – the only cuisine in the world to be named after a city rather than a region or an entire country – is the *Beisl*, a small, comfortable, usually family-run tavern, where people stand at the *Schank* (bar) with an *Achterl* (an eighth of a litre) of wine or a beer, waiting for a free table. There's usually a *Stammtisch* (a table reserved for regulars) too. This particular Viennese institution has been given a new lease of life, and there are several varieties, ranging from the genuine old *Wirtshaus* to the new and stylish *Edelbeisl*.

Just like the Viennese soul, the city's cuisine is a mixture of influences from the original member countries of the Habsburg monarchy, all absorbed by the imperial capital: the famed *Wiener Schnitzel* (traditionally veal, and served with potato salad) is actually of Byzantine descent, and the argument about whether Field Marshal Radetzky took the breadcrumbed speciality with him to Lombardy or returned to Vienna with the recipe for *costoletta milanese* still occupies the minds of food-lovers here as much as it ever has. *Gulasch* comes from Hungary (where it is referred to as *Pörkölt*), as does *Palatschinken*; the famous desserts *Marillenknödel*, *Apfelstrudel* and *Powidltascherln* are of Bohemian origin. Most dishes containing *Kraut* (cabbage) came from Poland originally, and even the very popular *Schinkenfleckerln* can't conceal the fact that it's descended from Italian pasta.

The Danube's equivalent of Paul Bocuse's nouvelle cuisine is called 'Neue Wiener Küche', a good combination of nouvelle cuisine and Viennese specialities robbed of their calories and adapted to contemporary needs. If you've never heard of *Tafelspitz*, *Surbraten*, *Golatsche* or *Vanillerostbraten*. Then now is the time to discover them: just sit down and order!

There are roughly 5,000 places to eat in Vienna, to suit every purse and every taste, ranging from the *Hassn* (a hot sausage eaten while standing up at a sausage stall) to the most sophisticated gourmet restaurant. The following selection gives some subjective tips for places that simply have to be tried if you want to get any real impression of the scene here in Vienna.

Restaurants

Viennese Cuisine

ZUR GOLDENEN GLOCKE
1050, Kettenbrückengasse 9.
Tel: 587 57 67.
Monday to Saturday 11am–2.30pm,
5.30pm–midnight.
Rustic Beisl with a beautiful garden.

GRÜNAUER
1070, Hermanngasse 32.
Tel: 526 40 80.
Friday to Tuesday 10am–3pm,
6pm–midnight.
Beisl with reasonably-priced traditional Viennese specialities. Best to
book a table.

ZU DEN DREI HACKEN
1010, Singerstrasse 28.
Tel: 512 58 95.
Monday to Friday 9am–midnight,
Saturday 10am–3pm.
Rustic Viennese restaurant.

ZUM HERKNER
1170, Dornbacher Strasse 123.
Tel: 45 43 86.
Monday to Friday 12am–2pm, 6–
9.30pm.
Beautiful old Edelbeisl, Schanigarten
in the summer. Book a table!

MARHOLD
1010, Fleischmarkt 9.
Tel: 533 28 73.
Monday to Friday 11am–11.30pm.
Large Beisl with generous portions of
reasonably-priced plain fare.

OFENLOCH
1010, Kurrentgasse 8.
Tel: 63 72 68.
Tuesday to Thursday 10am–midnight,
Friday, Saturday 10am–1am.
Traditional Viennese cuisine.

PFUDL
1010, Bäckerstrasse 22.
Tel: 512 67 05.
Monday to Friday 11.30am–11pm,
Saturday 3 –11pm.
Venerable old Edelbeisl.

ZUM SCHWARZEN ADLER
1050, Schönbrunner Strasse 40.
Tel: 55 71 74.
Monday 6pm–midnight, Tuesday to
Saturday 11am–3pm, 6pm–midnight,
On the expensive side; excellent fish
and meat specialities.

SMUTNY
1010, Elisa-
bethstrasse 8.
Tel: 587 13 56.
Open daily
9am–1am, food
served until
11.30pm.
Traditional Vi-
ennese cuisine.

STADTBEISL
1010, Nagler-
gasse 21.
Tel: 533 33 23.
Open daily 11
am–midnight.
Old Viennese Beisl; good-quality plain
fare in wood-panelled room.

City Heurige (taverns)

FIGLMÜLLER
1010, Wollzeile 5 (arcade).
Tel: 512 61 77.
Monday to Friday 8am–10.30pm,
Saturday 8am–3pm.
Gigantic portions of Schnitzel.

URBANI-KELLER
1010, Am Hof 12.
Tel: 63 91 02.
Open daily 6pm–1am.
Viennese and international cuisine.

Fish Restaurants

FISCHRESTAURANT WINTER
1110, Alberne Hafenzufahrtsstrasse 262. Tel: 76 23 17.
Tuesday to Saturday 12am–2.30pm, 6–10pm, Sunday 12am–2.30pm (closed on Sunday in July/August).
Excellent fish restaurant near the Danube with wonderful garden.

KORNAT
1010, Marc-Aurel-Strasse 8. Tel: 535 65 18.
Monday to Saturday 11am–3pm, 6pm–1am.
A small, simple restaurant at the edge of the Bermuda Triangle.

KERVANSARAY-HUMMER-BAR
1010, Mahlerstrasse 9. Tel: 512 88 43.
Monday to Saturday, and holidays, 12am–3pm, 6pm–1am.
Fine restaurant on the first floor of the 'Kervansaray'.

Gourmet Temples

ALTWIENERHOF
1150, Herklotzgasse 6. Tel: 83 71 45.
Monday to Friday 12am–2pm, 6.30–11pm, Saturday 6.30–11pm.
Top francophile cuisine; excellent wines; romantic winter garden.

ZU DEN DREI HUSAREN
1010, Weihburggasse 4. Tel: 512 10 92.
Open daily 12am–5pm, 6pm–midnight.
Old-established first-class restaurant with Viennese haute cuisine.

KORSO IM HOTEL BRISTOL
1010, Mahlerstrasse 2. Tel: 51 516 546.
Monday to Friday 12am–2pm, 7–11pm, Saturday 7–11pm.
Star chef Reinhard Gerer's exciting creations in an elegant atmosphere.

SCHWARZENBERG
1030, Schwarzenbergplatz 9. Tel: 78 45 15 0.
Open daily 12am–2.30pm, 6–11pm.
Elegant restaurant in the Palais Schwarzenberg; a beautiful view of the Schlosspark from the veranda.

SELINA
1080, Laudongasse 13. Tel: 42 64 04.
Monday to Saturday 12am–2pm, 6–11pm.
New Viennese cuisine.

STEIRERECK
1030, Rasumofskygasse 2. Tel: 713 31 68.
Monday to Friday 12am–3pm, 7–11.30pm.
New Viennese cuisine from one of the best cooks in the city.

'In' Restaurants

APROPOS
1010, Rudolfsplatz 12. Tel: 533 41 89.
Monday to Friday 10am–2pm, Saturday/Sunday 6pm–2am.
Restaurant for the 'in' scene.

CREPERIE AM SPITTELBERG
1070, Spittelbergggasse 12.
Tel: 96 15 70.
Open daily 6pm–midnight (Schanigarten until 10pm).
Cosy pub at the Spittelberg; French crêpes, health food.

DO & CO IM HAAS-HAUS
1010, Stephansplatz 12.
Tel: 535 39 69.
Monday to Saturday 12am–3pm, 6pm–1am.
Viennese cuisine, fish dishes, lobster and oysters, together with Vienna's most beautiful view.

PRINZ FERDINAND
1080, Bennoplatz 2.
Tel: 402 94 17.
Tuesday to Sunday 11am–midnight.
Pleasant little restaurant with light Viennese cuisine and excellent wine-list; delightful Schanigarten.

LUSTHAUS
1020, Prater, Freudenau 254.
Tel: 218 95 65.
Monday to Saturday 11am–11pm, Sunday 10am–11pm; in the wintertime only open at weekends.
Romantic pavilion; beautiful terrace, excellent food.

MA PITOM
1010, Seitenstettengasse 5.
Tel: 535 43 13.
Sunday to Thursday 5.30pm–1am, Friday, Saturday 5.30pm–2am.
Restaurant in the Bermuda Triangle; with Schanigarten.

OSWALD & KALB
1010, Bäckerstrasse 14.
Tel: 512 13 71.
Open daily 6pm–1am.
Viennese-Styrian specialities.

ECK
1070, Neustiftgasse/Zieglergasse.
Tel: 93 14 74.
Open daily 6pm–4am (closed on Sunday in the summer).
Popular restaurant serving Viennese cuisine.

ENRICO PANIGL
1080, Josefstädter Strasse 91.
Tel: 43 52 18.
Open daily 6pm–2am.
Nice old restaurant; large choice of pasta dishes; good wine list.

SALZAMT
1010, Ruprechtsplatz 1.
Tel: 533 53 32.
Open daily 5pm–1am.
The best restaurant in the Bermuda Triangle; meeting place of all 'in' people and those who like to think they are.

SANTO SPIRITO
1010, Kumpfgasse 7.
Tel: 512 99 98.
Open daily 6.30pm–2am.
Nice restaurant with music played at the table.

SCHNATTL
1080, Langegasse 40.
Tel: 42 34 00.
Monday to Friday 11.30am–2.30pm, 6pm–midnight, Saturday 11.30am–2.30pm.
Creative Viennese dishes.

STERN
1060, Gumpendorferstrasse 34.
Tel: 56 92 20.
Monday to Friday 11.30am–2am, Saturday, Sunday 5pm–2am.

Arabian

AL BADAUI
1010 Habsburgergasse 12a.
Tel: 533 79 25.
Open daily 6pm–midnight, in the summer also at midday.
Atmosphere from the Arabian Nights; fantastic starters.

Brazilian

MICHL'S CHURRASCARIA
1150, Sechshauserstrasse 76.
Tel: 83 01 96.
Open daily 6pm–midnight.
A large choice of meat dishes.

Chinese

KIANG
1010, Rotgasse 8.
Tel: 63 08 56.
Monday to Saturday 11.30am–2am, Sunday 6pm–1am.
Tasty dishes in the colourful plastic atmosphere of the 1960s.

IMPERIAL GARDENS
1010, Stubenring 18.
Tel: 512 49 11.
Monday to Saturday 12am–2.30pm, 7–11.30pm.
Vienna's most expensive Chinese restaurant serves Cantonese food and Peking duck.

French

ELSÄSSER GOURMANDISEN-MANUFAKTUR
1080, Albertgasse 19.
Tel: 408 70 67.

Restaurant: Tuesday to Friday evenings (reservations only).
Shop: Tuesday to Friday 10am–6.30pm, Saturday 10am–1pm.
Excellent pâté de fois gras.

Greek

DER GRIECHE PANOS TSATSARIS
1060, Barnabitengasse 5.
Tel: 587 74 66.
Open daily 11.30am–3pm, 6pm–midnight.
Regarded by Vienna's Greek community as the best in town.

SCHWARZE KATZE
1060, Girardigasse 6.
Tel: 587 06 25.
Tuesday to Sunday 6.30pm–1am.
A small restaurant.

Hungarian

ILONA-STÜBERL
1010, Bräunerstrasse 2.
Tel: 533 90 29.
Monday to Saturday 12am–3pm, 7–11pm.
Small restaurant with Hungarian specialities at a reasonable price.

Indian

MAHARADSCHA
1010, Gölsdorfgasse 1.
Tel: 63 74 43.
Open daily 12am–2.30pm, 6–11.30 pm.
The best Indian restaurant in town.

Italian

AL CAVALLINO
1010, Dorotheergasse 19.
Tel: 512 39 36.
Open daily 12am–3pm, 6pm–midnight.
Rustic atmosphere.

GROTTA AZZURRA
1010, Babenbergerstrasse 5.
Tel: 586 10 44.
Monday to Saturday 12am–3pm,
6pm–midnight.
Famous as Vienna's most up-market
Italian restaurant.

DA LUCIANO
1070, Sigmundsgasse 14.
Tel: 93 58 043.
Wednesday to Sunday 12am–3pm,
6pm–midnight.
Another high-class establishment in-
habited by the glitterati.

LA TAVERNETTA
1070, Burggasse 44.
Tel: 93 47 47.
Tuesday to Saturday 12am–2.30pm,
6.30–11pm.
Expensive.

OLIVA VERDE
1080, Florianigasse 15.
Tel: 42 41 06.
Monday to Friday 12am–3pm,
6pm–midnight.
Pleasant atmosphere; on the
health food side.

Japanese

K2
1010, Fleischmarkt 6.
Tel: 535 68 28.
Monday to Saturday 6pm–2am.
Vienna's best Sushi bar.

TENMAYA
1010, Krugerstrasse 3.
Tel: 512 73 97.
Open daily 11am–3pm, 5pm–mid-
night.
High-class Japanese restaurant with
excellent cuisine, Sushi bar und
Tatami rooms.

Jewish

ARCHE NOAH
1010, Judengasse 1b.
Tel: 533 13 74.
Monday to Friday 11.30am–3.30pm,
6.30–11pm, Saturday 11.30am–2.30
pm (November to April also 6.30–
11pm on Saturday).
In the Bermuda Triangle.

Korean

OSTWIND
1070, Lindengasse 24.
Tel: 93 41 82.
Daily 11.30am–3pm, 5.30pm–midnight.
Reasonably-priced Korean, Chinese
and Japanese specialities.

Mexican

MARGARITAVILLE
1010, Bartensteingasse 3.
Tel: 42 47 86.
Monday to Saturday 6pm–2am, Sunday 6pm–midnight.

Russian

FEUERVOGEL
1090, Alserbachstrasse 21.
Tel: 34 10 392.
Monday to Saturday 6.30pm–1am.
This elegant restaurant has been Vienna's top Russian establishment for over 70 years.

Serbian

BEOGRAD
1040, Schikanedergasse 5.
Tel: 587 74 44.
Thursday to Tuesday 11.30am–4am
Balkan specialities until the early hours of the morning; garden open until 10pm.

Spanish

PEDRO'S MESON
1070, Siebensterngasse 5.
Tel: 93 99 85.
Monday to Saturday 6pm–1am.
Small and cosy.

Turkish

LEVANTE
1080, Josefstädterstrasse 14.
Tel: 408 53 06.
1010, Wallnerstrasse 2.
Tel: 533 23 26.
Both establishments open daily 11.30am–11.30pm.
Kebab and vegetable specialities.

KEBABHAUS
1040, Operngasse 26.
Tel: 587 53 08.
Open daily 11.30am–11.30pm.
Kebab specialities; take-away service.

Vegetarian

WRENKH
1010, Bauernmarkt 10.
Tel: 533 15 26, 535 33 62 (Bar).
Restaurant: Monday to Saturday 11.30am–2.30pm, 6pm–midnight.
Bar: 11am–1am.
Vienna's best vegetarian restaurant; elegant wall-panelling.

Coffee-Houses

See also *Coffee-Houses* itinerary

ALT WIEN
1010, Bäckerstrasse 9.
Tel: 512 52 22.
Monday to Friday 10am–4am, Saturday, Sunday 3pm–4am.

BRÄUNERHOF
1010, Stallburggasse 2.
Tel: 512 38 93.
Monday to Friday 7.30am–7.30pm, Saturday 7.30am–6pm, Sunday 10 am–6pm.

CENTRAL
1010, Herrengasse 14
(Palais Ferstel).
Tel: 535 41 76.
Monday to Saturday 9am–8pm.

DIGLAS
1010, Wollzeile 10.
Tel: 512 84 01.
Monday to Saturday 7am–midnight, Sunday and holidays 10am–midnight.

FRAUENHUBER
1010, Himmelpfortgasse 6.
Tel: 512 43 23.
Monday to Friday 8am–11pm, Saturday 8am–4pm.

GRIENSTEIDL
1010 Michaelerplatz 2.
Tel: 535 26 92.
Open daily 8am–midnight.

HAWELKA
1010, Dorotheergasse 12.
Tel: 512 82 30.
Monday, Wednesday to Saturday 8am–2am, Sunday and holidays 4pm–2am.

KLEINES CAFÉ
1010, Franziskanerplatz 3.
Monday to Saturday 10am–2am, Sunday 1pm–2am.

LANDTMANN
1010, Dr Karl-Lueger-Ring 4.
Tel: 63 91 28.
Open daily 8am–midnight.

MUSEUM
1010, Friedrichstrasse 6.
Tel: 56 52 02.
Open daily 7am–11pm.

SALZGRIES
1010, Marc-Aurel-Strasse 6.
Tel: 533 54 26.
Monday to Friday 8am–1am, Saturday, Sunday and holidays 12am–1am.

SPERL
1060, Gumpendorfer Strasse 11.
Tel: 56 41 58.
Monday to Saturday 7am–11pm, Sunday 3–11pm.

Snacks

LUSTIG ESSEN
1150, Hütteldorferstrasse 4.
Tel: 92 51 63.
Monday to Saturday 11.30am–11pm. Viennese and international specialities in mini portions; the best thing to do is simply to eat your way through the menu.

TRZESNIEWSKI
1010, Dorotheergasse 1.
Tel: 512 32 91.
Monday to Friday 9am–7.30pm, Saturday 9am–1pm (every first Saturday in the month until 6pm.)
Bread rolls with spicy spreads.

'In' Bars

Vienna's nightlife begins late, but that makes it all the more intensive. Here is a choice of the most important establishments:

REISS CHAMPAGNERTREFF
1010, Marco d'Aviano-Gasse 1.
Tel: 512 71 98.
Sunday to Friday 11am–3am, Saturday 10am–3am.

CAFÉ-BAR IN DER SEZESSION
1010, Friedrichstrasse 12.
Tel: 56 93 86.
Open daily 10am–2am.
Colourful downstairs pub.

EDEN
1010, Liliengasse 2.
Tel: 512 74 50.
Open daily 11pm–4am.
Vienna's nicest Plüschbar.

DIE BAR
1010, Sonnenfelsgasse 9.
Tel: 513 14 99.
Open daily 9pm–4am.
Good stand-up bar; large choice of drinks and cocktails.

HOLD
1010, Biberstrasse 8.
Tel: 512 61 29.
Wednesday to Monday 8pm–2am.
Pink meeting place for the 'in' scene.

ENGLÄNDER
1010, Postgasse 2.
Tel: 512 27 34.
Monday to Saturday 8am–2am, Sunday and holidays 10am–2am.
Retreat for fans of 'Oswald & Kalb'.

OSWALD & KALB
1010, Bäckerstrasse 14.
Tel: 512 13 71.
Monday to Thursday 4.30pm–2am, Friday 4.30pm–4am, Saturday 6pm–4am, Sunday 6pm–2am.
As popular as ever.

SALZAMT
1010, Ruprechtsplatz 1.
Tel: 533 53 32.
Open daily 5pm–4am.
Superbly-designed pub in the Bermuda Triangle.

WUNDER-BAR
1010, Schönlaterngasse 8.
Tel: 512 79 89.
Open daily 4pm–2am.

Live Music

ROTER ENGEL
1010, Rabensteig 5.
Tel: 535 41 05.
Monday to Wednesday 3pm–2am, Thursday to Saturday 3pm–4am, Sunday and holidays 5pm–2am.
Design by Coop Himmelblau; daily live music; billiards.

JAZZLAND
1010, Franz Josephs-Kai 29.
Tel: 533 25 75.
Monday to Saturday 7pm–2am.
Daily live jazz from 9pm; hot dishes and snacks.

OPUS ONE
1010, Mahlerstrasse 11.
Tel: 513 20 75.
Jazz.

PAPAS TAPAS
1040, Schwarzenbergplatz 10.
Tel: 505 03 11.
Sunday to Thursday 8pm–2am, Friday, Saturday 8pm–4am.
Large pub with *tapas* and live music.

Nightclubs

P1
1010, Rotgasse 9.
Tel: 535 99 95.
Open daily 9pm–4am.
The largest inner-city disco.

U4
*1120, Schönbrunnerstrasse 222
(U4 Parkshop Meidling).*
Tel: 85 83 07.
Open daily 9pm–4am.
Disco with 'underground' touch.

NACHTWERK
*1232, Dr Gonda-Gasse 9/
Laxenburgerstrasse.*
Tel: 616 88 80.
Monday to Thursday 8pm–4am,
Friday, Saturday 8pm–5am.
Large disco on the edge of town;
lasers, 16,000-watt sound system
and giant video screen.

VOLKSGARTEN
1010, Volksgarten (U3).
Tel: 63 05 18.
Monday 10pm–5am, Tuesday, Wednesday 10pm–4am, Thursday 8pm–
2am, Friday, Saturday 8pm–5am,
Sunday 5pm–4am.
1950s atmosphere; dancing outside in
the summer; Monday night special,
'Soul Seduction'.

QUEEN ANNE
1010, Johannesgasse 12.
Tel: 512 02 03.
Open daily 9pm–5am.
Beautiful people; cocktail bar.

Cabaret

METROPOL
1170, Hernalser Hauptstrasse 55.
Tel: 43 35 43.
Cabaret and music programmes; open-
air theatre in the summer.

SPEKTAKEL
1050, Hamburgerstrasse 14.
Tel: 587 06 23.
Cabaret and Beisl.

KULISSE
1170, Rosensteingasse 39.
Tel: 45 38 70.
Cabaret and music programme; cosy
Beisl with Viennese cuisine.

NIEDERMAIR
1080, Lenaugasse 1a.
Tel: 408 44 92.
Young cabaret and satire; 'Kabarett-
beisl Niedermeierei' is next door (daily
from 6pm; Tel: 408 92 93).

Eating for Night Owls

SALZ & PFEFFER
1060, Joanelligasse 8.
Tel: 56 92 77.
Open daily 7pm–8am, Friday, Satur-
day 7pm–9am.
Plain fare and international cuisine.

CAFÉ DRECHSLER
1060, Linke Wienzeile 22.
Tel: 587 85 80.
Monday to Friday 4am–8pm, Satur-
day 4am–6pm.
Mixed public, simple cuisine.

You can also satisfy your appetite until midnight in Apropos, Salzamt,
Oswald & Kalb, Eck and Stern.

TRAVEL ESSENTIALS

When to Visit

The temperature can fluctuate between 15 and 35 degrees Centigrade in August, and between plus 5 and minus 22 degrees in January. The one thing you can rely on unfailingly is the wind: it blows at least 200 days a year. Normally, spring and autumn are the best times of year for a visit to Vienna. The clear light in autumn, after the summer haze, is particularly beautiful. Rain protection and a warmish jacket are always a good idea whatever the season.

Driving in the City

In Vienna, the same applies as for other large cities: leave your car in the hotel garage! And above all, make sure you avoid the city centre within the Ringstrasse; even taxi drivers have a great deal of trouble coping with the continually changing system of one-way streets. The section entitled 'Getting Around' also contains information on how you can reach the city centre from the various *autobahns*.

By Train

Vienna has two main railway stations: the Westbahnhof and the Südbahnhof.

Westbahnhof
1150, Mariahilfergürtel/Mariahilferstrasse (U6, Tram Nos 5,6,9,18) for all destinations in Western Austria, Germany, France, Switzerland, etc.

Südbahnhof
1040, Wiener Gürtel 1 (Bus 13A, U1, S-Bahn, Tram Nos O, D, 18) for destinations in Southern Austria, Italy, the former Yugoslavia, etc.

Bahnhof Wien-Mitte
1030, Landstrasser Hauptstrasse (S-Bahn, U4, U3, Tram O, Bus 74A) for destinations in the north and northeast.

Wien-Nord/Praterstern
1020, Praterstern (U1, S-Bahn, Tram Nos 1, 5, O, Bus 80A) for connections to Northern Austria.

Franz-Josephs-Bahnhof
1090, Julius-Tandler-Platz 9 (Trams D, 5, near the U4). This station has lost a lot of its former importance; most departures from here are to Eastern Austria and Czechoslovakia.

As well as in the stations themselves, seats can be reserved in the city centre at the Österreichische

Verkehrsbüro, or Austrian Tourist Office (1010, Operngasse 3, Monday to Friday 8.30am–5.30pm); the Südbahnhof and the Westbahnhof also have a Bahnhofsreisebüro, or station travel office, which looks after things like bookings, tickets, timetables, etc.

'Bahntotalservice'
Tel: 17 00 (daily 4am–10pm)
Central Train Information
Tel: 17 17

By Air

Wien-Schwechat airport lies roughly 17km (10 miles) south-east of Vienna. It was built in 1960 and has been undergoing extension work since the end of the 1980s.

By car it takes around 30 minutes to get from the city centre to the airport, via Franz-Josephs-Kai and the airport *autobahn*, but the early morning and evening traffic jams before the *autobahn* itself can increase the time considerably.

Departure from the City Air Terminal, Hilton-Stadtpark (near the U3, U4), daily 5am–7.30am and 7.30pm–midnight every 30 minutes, 7.30am–7.30pm every 20 minutes. Journey time: 30–50 minutes. There are also airport buses from the Westbahnhof and the Südbahnhof (departure, hourly; Journey time approximately 50 minutes; price for both services is 50 öS).

Since the airport is outside the city itself taxis can be rather expensive as the trip back also has to be paid for (roughly 350–400öS). A few radio taxis – eg 31 300 – give discounts if a taxi is ordered to arrive at the airport in advance (from 270öS).

Airport Post Office: Open daily, 7.30am–8pm

MONEY MATTERS

In general the banks are open Monday to Friday 8am–12.30pm and 1.30–3pm (Thursday until 5.30pm). The head offices of several financial institutions stay open at lunchtime, too (eg Creditanstalt, 1010, Schottengasse 1; Erste Österreichische, 1010, Graben 21; Zentralsparkasse, 1030, Vordere Zollamtsstrasse 13). There is also a comprehensive network of automatic teller machines.
Südbahnhof: Daily 7am–10pm
Westbahnhof: Daily 7am–10pm
Airport: Daily 6am–10pm
Air Terminal/Hilton Hotel: Daily 8am–12.30pm and 2–6pm
ÖAMTC Touring Centre West: Currency exchange daily 7am–6pm (1140, Hadikgasse 128, in the direction of the Westautobahn).
Currency Exchange: Stephansplatz (daily 9am–5.30pm), Opernpassage (daily 8am–7pm)
Automatic tellers in the city centre:
Stephansplatz 2
Kärntner Strasse 51 (opposite the Staatsoper)
Franz-Josephs-Kai 21/Schwedenplatz
Schottengasse 10

USEFUL INFORMATION

Geography and Topography

Austria's federal capital of Vienna is also the smallest of the country's nine federal states and has 1.6 million inhabitants. The city lies at 16 degrees 21' 42" east and 48 degrees 14' 54" north. As far as its landscape is concerned, the west of Vienna belongs to the Northern Vienna Woods, then come the mountainous Alpine foothills, the Viennese tableland, the

Danube meadows and the flat alluvial plain of the Marchfeld. The north, including the Bisamberg, is already part of Weinviertler Hügelland. Vienna lies at an average of 172 metres (564ft) above sea-level; the highest point is the Hermannskogel (542 metres/1,778ft) in the north-west, and the lowest point is in the Lobau by the Danube (150 metres/490ft).

The surface area of the city is approximately 414.5km² (160 square miles), roughly half of which (80 square miles) is under the plough. A walk round the city's borders would be roughly 130km (80 miles) long.

Districts

1. Innere Stadt 2. Leopoldstadt 3. Landstrasse 4. Wieden 5. Margareten 6. Mariahilf 7. Neubau 8. Josefstadt 9. Alsergrund 10. Favoriten 11. Simmering 12. Meidling 13. Hietzing 14. Penzing 15. Rudolfsheim-Fünfhaus 16. Ottkaring 17. Hernals 18. Währing 19. Döbling 20. Brigittenau 21. Floridsdorf 22. Donaustadt 23. Liesing

Climate and Viewing Points

Vienna lies on the border between the continental temperate climate and the oceanic climate. The average temperature is minus 1.4 degrees Centigrade in January (when temperatures can vary between minus 22 and plus 5), and 19 degrees Centigrade at the height of the summer (variations from 15 to 35 degrees). Roughly 600mm (23½ inches) of rain fall annually, but it is spread throughout the seasons relatively uniformly.

On clear days, especially in spring and late autumn, the following places will give you the best views of Vienna:

Leopoldsberg: 425m (1,400ft), the northernmost part of the Kahlenberg range; the medieval fortress tower on the summit, restored after 1945, provides a wonderful view of Vienna and the Danube.

Kahlenberg: The 484-m (1,587-ft) high neighbouring mountain of the Leopoldsberg affords a magnificent view of the city (observation terrace).

Hermannskogel: This mountain, the highest point in Vienna (542m/1,778ft), lies to the north-west of the city; there's a great view of the city to be had from up here, too.

Donauturm: To the north of the Danube, the Donaupark and the 252-metre (826-ft) high Donauturm (Danube Tower) were constructed as part of the International Garden Exhibition in 1964; the top floor, which revolves, contains a café, and also a restaurant which isn't all that great – but the view is magnificent.

St Stephen's Cathedral/Stephansplatz: Access to the express lift up to the Nordturm (North Tower) is in the left side-aisle of the Cathedral;

open daily from 9am–6pm. Access to the Südturm (South Tower) which is 137m (450ft) high is on the outside of the Cathedral; open daily 9am–5.30pm.

Haas-Haus/Stephansplatz: The café on the seventh floor provides the finest view of the colourful roof-tiles of the Cathedral. There is also a particularly fine view to be had from the terrace of the restaurant next door, Do & Co (unfortunately only accessible to restaurant guests).

Vienna and Foreigners

The Viennese's attitude to foreigners is double-edged. He likes them in small doses and is also happy to provide them with information – though it's not always quite accurate. Large concentrations of tourists make him nervous, especially if they happen to be linked arm in arm, carousing loudly. In this kind of situation you might hear the derogatory word for a German *(Piefke)* or something even worse leave his lips.

GETTING AROUND

Maps

Most bookstores and kiosks in the city centre sell small plans of the city and guides to Vienna. There's a particularly comprehensive selection of maps and city guides at **Freytag & Berndt**, 1010, Kohlmarkt 9.

Round Trips

CITYRAMA SIGHTSEEING REISEBÜRO
1010, Börsegasse 1, Tel: 534 13-0

Round Trips by Boat

Between the end of March and the end of October the DDSG *(Donaudampfschiffahrtsgesellschaft)* offers a variety of round trips and outings by boat.

For information contact: DDSG, 1020, Handelskai 265, Tel: 217 10 0.

Fiaker (Horse-Drawn Cabs)

The Viennese *fiaker* were at their most popular in the 18th and 19th centuries: at that time there were more than 1,000 of these picturesque horse-drawn cabs in the city. Around three dozen of them remain today, and they are mainly used to give tourist rides through the city centre. Just as with the gondoliers in Venice it is recommended that you agree on a fixed price before starting your journey; the main 'cab ranks' can be found on the Heldenplatz and on Stephansplatz.

Guided Tours

For those interested in the less well-known aspects of Vienna, the programme known as *Wiener Stadtspaziergänge*, or 'Walks through Vienna', offers over three dozen different routes on various themes, such as 'Crime Legends of Old Vienna', 'The Vienna of *The Third Man*', 'Jugendstil', or 'On the Trail of Mozart'. Each tour is accompanied by a trained guide, costs around 100 *schilling* and takes about 90 minutes to complete. A free brochure on these tours can be found at Tourist Information (1010, Kärntnerstrasse 38).

In the summer months the *Reisebuchladen* (Travel Book Shop) organises alternative guided tours of Vienna with a critical edge (information: 1090 Kolingasse 6, Tel: 34 33 84).

Public Transport

The quickest way to get around is to take one of the five U-Bahn lines. Trams and buses can result in waits in the early morning and the evening, and after 8pm. The trams and the U-Bahn generally start at 5am and go on until midnight, while the buses (apart from the City-Buses) start at 6.30am and go on until midnight. The so-called City-Buses in District 1 are a very comfortable way to travel. A disadvantage, though, is that they only run until 8pm on weekdays, and

until just 2pm on Saturdays (although on the first Saturday of every month and on the four Saturdays before Christmas they run until 5pm).

Night Buses

On the nights preceding national holidays and Sundays, eight night bus routes run between 12.30am and 4am from Schwedenplatz. The good news: it's a great way of getting home cheaply in the middle of the night. The bad news: the journey time is relatively long, because the buses have to go right round all the most important districts.

A one-way-trip costs 25öS, and the tickets have to be bought from automatic machines in the buses themselves. Precise times of departure and routing, etc are available in a free brochure that can be obtained at information centres of the Wiener Verkehrsbetrieb (eg U-Bahn station Karlsplatz, Monday to Friday daily 7am–6pm, Saturday, Sunday, public holidays 8.30am–4pm).

Tickets & Travel Regulations

The various forms of public transport are all part of the VOR (Verkehrsverbund Ostregion). This means that you can use just one ticket to travel by bus, U-Bahn, tram and S-Bahn, the condition being that you mustn't break your journey for any length of time, and must always travel in one logical direction.

Single tickets cost 20öS and are sold on buses and trams as well as from automatic machines in U-Bahn and S-Bahn stations.

A cheaper way of doing things is to buy so-called *Vorverkaufsfahrscheine* and *Spezialfahrscheine*, advance tickets and special tickets sold in most tobacconist shops (Tabak Trafik) and the advance sales outlets of the Wiener Verkehrsbetrieb.

Advance sales outlets:
1010, U-Bahn station Stephansplatz
1010, U-Bahn station Karlsplatz
1010, U-Bahn station Schwedenplatz
(Opening times: Monday 6am–6pm, Tuesday–Friday 6.30am–6.30pm)

Ticket prices:
Vorverkaufsfahrschein: 75öS (can only be bought in blocks of five at a time).
8-Tage-Umwelt-Streifennetzkarte: 235öS (valid for 8 days and can also be used by more than one person).
Netzkarte 72 Stunden Wien: 115öS (for as many trips as you like within 72 hours).
Netzkarte 24 Stunden Wien: 45öS (for as many trips as you like within 24 hours).
Schnupperkarte: 35öS (For as many trips as you like during the same day between the hours of 8am and 8pm).

Taxis

It's basically no problem to get hold of a taxi in Vienna – either wave one down or go to one of the taxi-ranks. Delays are only likely to occur in the morning and evening rush hour, in rainy or icy weather and also during the Ball Season (January to February) between midnight and 2am. There's a list of all the city's taxi-rank locations on page three of the Vienna phone book.

Prices: Within the Gürtel trips cost between 50 and 80 *schilling*; and there's an extra charge for luggage as well as during the evening and at weekends. Fixed basic charge: 22öS.

Radio-Taxis:
Tel: 60 160
Tel: 31 300
Tel: 91 011
Tel: 40 100

There is also an extra charge of 10öS made if you order a cab by telephone, though the distance it travels to reach you (minus waiting time) is free of charge.

For taxi rides to the **airport** it's a good idea to say that the radio-taxi has to go 'zum Flughafen' because several of the city's cab companies have a special discount rate here.

Courier Services:

Blitzkurier: Tel: 34 65 05

Fahrradbotendienst Veloce (bicycle couriers): Tel: 505 12 12

Most taxis will also accept express packages.

Cycling

Vienna has over 300km (180 miles) of cycle paths, though the cycle lanes and part of the pavement reserved for pedestrians are not always very clearly delineated, especially in the area around the Ringstrasse and along the Donaukanal. Cyclists and pedestrians should keep a sharp eye out for one another. The cycle paths in the Lobau and through the Prater are particularly attractive, as are the ones along the Donaukanal and the Danube.

A brochure listing cycle paths is available from **Stadtinformation** (1080, Town Hall, entrance on Friedrich-Schmidt-Platz, Monday to Friday 6am–6pm; Tel: 403 89 89).

On the U-Bahn system it's possible to travel with a bicycle on Saturdays from 4pm onwards and all day long on Sundays and public holidays; also from May to September, Monday to Friday 9am–3pm and from 6.30pm onwards, and also from 9am onwards on Saturdays.

Bicycle Hire: 1010, Salztorbrücke, Tel: 31 12 58

1020, Prater (near the Hochschaubahn), Tel: 26 01 65

22, Donauinsel Süd (next to the Steinspornbrücke), Tel: 22 05 9911

On Foot

All the major sights within the Ringstrasse can easily be visited on foot. The Kärntnerstrasse, the Graben, the Kohlmarkt, the Naglergasse and the Blutgasse are all pedestrian precincts, as is the Spittelberg. But beware: delivery lorries are allowed to drive along these streets until 11am daily.

Hotels

Whether you choose to spend the night in Vienna's top luxury hotel, the Palais Schwarzenberg, or would prefer a little *Pension*, there's sure to be something to suit your taste. The following is just a brief selection.

5-Star Luxury Hotels

All Vienna's traditional luxury hotels are situated either on or very near the Ringstrasse:

HOTEL IM PALAIS SCHWARZENBERG
1030, Schwarzenbergplatz 9.
Tel: 78 45 15.
38 rooms; double rooms from 4100öS (facing the park: from 4800öS)
Regal accommodation, in a wing of a baroque palace; some rooms have views of the magnificent private park.

HOTEL BRISTOL
1010 Kärntner Ring 1, Tel: 515 160.
146 rooms; double rooms from 4320öS.
Famous Ringstrasse hotel next to the Opera House, with the best hotel restaurant in Vienna.

International Hotel Chains

VIENNA INTER-CONTINENTAL
1030, Johannesgasse 28.
Tel: 711 22-0.
195 rooms; doubles from 2480öS.

HILTON
1030, Am Stadtpark. Tel: 717 00.
600 rooms; doubles from 2590öS.

VIENNA MARRIOTT
1010, Parkring 12a. Tel: 515 18-0.
316 rooms; doubles from 3800öS.
Postmodern architecture, opposite
the Stadtpark.

4-Star Hotels

SCANDIC CROWN HOTEL
1020, Handelskai 269. Tel: 217 77.
367 rooms; doubles from 2550öS.
A former grain silo on the Danube,
converted into a hotel (terrace with
view of river).

BIEDERMEIER HOTEL IM SÜNNHOF
1030, Landstrasser Haupstrasse 28,
Tel: 75 55 75.
204 rooms; doubles from 2150öS.
Peacefully situated hotel in a restored
Biedermeier building.

THEATER-HOTEL JOSEFSTADT
1080, Josefstädterstrasse 22.
Tel: 42 36 48.
54 rooms; doubles from 1400öS.
Attractive hotel, next to theatre of
the same name, only a few minutes
away from the Ring.

KÖNIG VON UNGARN
1010, Schulerstrasse 10.
Tel: 515 84-0.
33 rooms; doubles from 1850öS.
Small traditional hotel in an originally medieval building near the
Stephansplatz.

3-Star Hotels and below

HOTEL WANDL
1010, Petersplatz 9, Tel: 534 55-0.
138 rooms; doubles from 1350öS.
Small and comfortable hotel behind
the Peterskirche, near the Graben
pedestrian precinct.

HOTELPENSION ZIPSER
1080 Lange Gasse 49, Tel: 42 02 28.
50 rooms; doubles from 1280öS.
Nice family hotel only a few minutes'
walk from the *Rathaus* (Town Hall).

Pensions

ARENBERG
1010, Stubenring 2, Tel: 512 52 91.
25 rooms; doubles from 1280öS.
Comfortable 4-star *Pension* (Vienna's
Pensionen are star-rated) near the
Urania.

NOSSEK
1010, Graben 17, Tel: 533 70 41.
26 rooms; doubles from 850öS.
There are probably nicer *Pensionen*
in the city, but none so beautifully
located at this price.

Campsites

WIEN-WEST II
1140, Hüttelbergstrasse 80.
Tel: 94 23 14.
Open from April–October

WIEN-SÜD
1230, Breitenfurter Strasse 269.
Tel: 86 92 18.
Open from May–September

Camping Information

CAMPING UND CARAVANING CLUB AUSTRIA (CCA)
1150, Mariahilferstrasse 180.
Tel: 85 35 35-0.

Youth Hostels

TURMHERBERGE DON BOSCO
1030, Lechnerstrasse 12.
Tel: 713 14 94.
43 beds (rooms have more than one bed). One night without breakfast from 55öS.
Near the Prater and the Donaukanal, not central, but extremely cheap.

JUGENDHERBERGE MYRTHENGASSE
1070, Myrthengasse 7, Tel: 93 63 16.
225 beds, bed & breakfast from 130öS.
A comfortable youth hostel, near the Spittelberg.

SCHLOSSHERBERGE AM WILHELMINENBERG
1160, Savoyenstrasse 2.
Tel: 458 50 30.
164 beds (4-bed-rooms), bed & breakfast from 170öS.
A superb youth hostel on the edge of the city, in the middle of a castle park; close to the Vienna Woods.

BUSINESS HOURS & HOLIDAYS

Shop opening times in Vienna are a continually recurring bone of contention, disturbing the otherwise smooth partnership between employers' and employees' representatives. Since 1991 the shops have been allowed to remain open Monday to Friday until 7.30pm and once a week until 9pm, and until 5pm on one Saturday every month. Despite this, a large number of shops in Vienna continue to open only until 6pm or 6.30pm on weekdays, until 12 noon or 12.30pm on Saturdays and until 5pm on the first Saturday in every month, just as they have always done. Most supermarkets and grocery stores stick to these times too. Exceptions are the Meinl-Gourmet chain on the Opernring which stays open daily until 8pm, and the Billa supermarket chain which stays open until 8pm every Friday and until 1pm every Saturday. Most shops in the city stay open over lunchtime, and many of them remain open until 8pm on Thursdays.

On the last four Saturdays before Christmas, almost every shop is open until 5pm.

Public Holidays
The only public holidays mentioned here are the ones that could take place on weekdays:
New Year's Day: 1 January
Epiphany: 6 January

Easter Monday
Labour Day *(Staatsfeiertag)*: 1 May
Ascension Day *(Christi Himmelfahrt)*
Whit Monday *(Pfingstmontag)*
Corpus Christi *(Fronleichnam)*
Assumption *(Mariä Himmelfahrt)*
National Holiday *(Nationalfeiertag)* 26 October
All Saints' Day *(Allerheiligen)*: 1st November
Immaculate Conception *(Mariä Empfängnis)*: 8 December

Christmas Day *(1. Weihnachtstag)*:
25 December
St Stephen's Day *(2. Weihnachtstag)*:
26 December

MEDIA

Newspapers & Magazines

The Austrian newspaper market is one of the most comprehensive in the world. The largest-selling daily paper in the country is the tabloid known as the *Kronen-Zeitung*. The 'Krone', as it is familiarly called, is read by over 40 per cent of Austrians (3 million readers out of a 7.5 million population), making it one of the most popular newspapers anywhere in the world. Second, with a readership of almost 15 per cent, is the *Kurier* daily paper, which has been limping along behind the *Krone* with less and less success for years now, while affecting a kind of upper middle-class grandeur. The German *WAZ* (*Westdeutsche Allgemeine Zeitung*) has a 45 per cent stake in both.

German capital (in the shape of the Springer firm) also plays a role in the *Standard* newspaper, which started at the end of the 1980s. This one, printed on salmon-pink paper, is aimed at a liberal-intellectual readership.

The upper middle-class and very conservative *Presse*, with its motto *Auch der Kopf braucht sein Frühstück* (literally: 'Give your brains some breakfast too'), and its perpetual moaning about the 'decline of the Western world', is struggling with se-

vere financial problems. The only other paper worth mentioning is the *Wiener Zeitung*, the official newspaper of the Austrian Republic.

The *Falter* was founded as a city magazine and, as a discussion forum, it is left-wing alternative in its approach. It also contains the best 'What's On' guide.

Cultural events are also announced in the daily papers (especially in the Saturday editions).

Television & Radio

ORF, the Austrian radio and television concern, monopolises the country's media and the political parties feel justified in intervening quite calmly at the highest level where personnel questions are involved. Quite often, ministerial secretaries are given high posts in the ORF, and vice-versa. Top jobs at Tele 5, RTL and Premiere are firmly in private hands.

The ORF has two TV stations (**FS 1** and **FS 2**) and four radio stations (**Ö1** with the emphasis on classical music, **Ö2** with regional programmes, **Ö3** with pop music, and also the foreign-language station **Blue Danube Radio**, on 103.8 FM, which carries news in English at 7am, midday and 6pm. Private radio stations have discovered a few loopholes recently – **Radio CD**, for example, broadcasts to Vienna from nearby Bratislava.

Many homes in Vienna have cable TV, and a choice of more than two dozen channels.

POST & TELECOMMUNICATIONS

Post offices are generally open Monday to Friday 8am–noon and 2–6pm (financial transactions can only take place until 5pm), and the main post office in each of the districts is also open on Saturdays from 8am to 10am (again, no financial transactions).

Main Post Offices

Head Post Office: 1010, Fleischmarkt 19; daily 24 hours.
Postamt Börse: daily 24 hours
Südbahnhof: daily 24 hours
Westbahnhof: daily 24 hours
Franz-Josephs-Bahnhof: daily 24 hours
Airport: daily 7am–7.30pm

Telephoning

Vienna has a comprehensive network of modern phone boxes, which take 1, 5, 10 and 20 *schilling* coins.

Dialling internationally is straightforward. The international access code from Austria is 00. After this, dial the relevant country code: Australia (61); Canada (1); Germany (49); Italy (39); Japan (81); the Netherlands (31); Spain (34); United Kingdom (44); United States (1). If you are using a US phone credit card, dial the company's access number as follows: AT&T, Tel: 022-903-011; MCI, Tel: 022-903-012; Sprint, Tel: 022-903-014.

SPECIAL SERVICES

Disabled People

CITY INFORMATION
(STADTINFORMATION)
1080, Rathaus (Town Hall; Entrance on Friedrich-Schmidt-Platz)
Tel: 403 89 89
Monday to Friday 8am–6pm

CLUB 21
1140, Linzerstrasse 466
Tel: 97 58 44 (Frau Nüchtern)
Monday to Friday 3pm–7pm

For Children

BABYSITTER-ZENTRALE
1160, Herbststrasse 6–10
Tel: 491 23
Monday to Friday 7am–3pm

ÖSTERREICHISCHER AKADEMISCHER
GÄSTEDIENST/BABYSITTERZENTRALE
1040, Mühlgasse 20
Tel: 587 35 25
Monday to Thursday 9am–5pm, Friday 9am–3pm

Open-air Swimming Pools for Children & Forest Playgrounds
Brochures available free of charge from **Stadtinformation**, 1080, Rathaus (Town Hall; Entrance on Friedrich-Schmidt-Platz). Tel: 403 89 89. Monday to Friday 8am–6pm.
Swimming Pool Information Service: 601 120
Swimming Pool Answerphone Service: 15 35

HOLIDAY GAMES (FERIENSPIEL)
Tel: 4000 then dial 84400 direct (information)

ARLEQUIN MARIONETTENTHEATER
(PUPPET THEATRE)
1090, Seegasse 28
Tel: 341 90 43

URANIA PUPPENSPIELE
(PUPPET THEATRE)
1010, Uraniastrasse 1
Tel: 712 61 91

TRITTBRETTL
1160, Haberlgasse 91
Tel: 408 57 13
Children's cabaret and puppet theatre

MOKI – MOBILE THEATRE FOR
CHILDREN
1040, Blechturmgasse 12–13
Tel: 505 98 06

Pavement bingo

For Women

Frauencafé
1080, Langegasse 11
Tel: 43 37 54

Frauenkommunikation-szentrum im WUK
1090, Währingerstrasse 59
Tel: 408 50 57

Frauenhaus
Tel: 31 56 56, 319 56 56

Gays/Lesbians

Autonomes Lesbenzentrum
1090, Währingerstrasse 59, Stiege VI
Tel: 408 50 57

HOSI – Homosexuelle Initiative Wien
1020, Novaragasse 40
Tel: 26 66 04

Rosa-Lila-Villa
1060, Linke Wienzeile 102
Tel: 56 81 50

USEFUL ADDRESSES

Tourist Information

Wiener Fremdenverkehrsverband
1025, Obere Augartenstrasse 40.
Tel: 211 14-0;
Monday to Friday 8am–4pm

Those arriving in Vienna by car will find initial information, brochures, city maps and help in finding accommodation at the exits from the *autobahns*: **Tourist Information Auhof/ Wien West** at the exit ('Ausfahrt') from the Westautobahn A1; April to Oct daily 8am–10pm, Jan to March daily 10am–6pm
Tourist Information Süd on the Südautobahn A2; at the exit marked Zentrum/Triesterstrasse; April to June, Oct: 9am–7pm, July to Sept 8am–10pm
Tourist Information at the Airport
Arrivals Hall; Jan–May 8.30am–10pm, June–Sept 8.30am–11pm, Oct–Dec 8.30am–10pm
Tourist Information in the Centre
1010, Kärntnerstrasse 38, daily 9am–7pm; Tel: 513 88 92.
City Information (Stadtinformation)
1080, Town Hall, entrance on Friedrich-Schmidt-Platz, Tel: 403 89 89; Monday – Friday 8am–6pm
Austrobus: Opernpassage (between the exit 'Oper' and the exit 'Kärntnerstrasse'), daily 9am–7pm (Hotel information, currency exchange, theatre tickets, sightseeing tours).

Overseas Information

Austrian Tourist Office
500 5th Avenue, #2009-2022
New York, NY 10110
Tel: 212 944 6885
Fax: 212 730 4568

Austrian Tourist Office
30 St George St., London WIR OAL
Tel: 071 629 0461
Fax: 071 499 6038

Banks

Z-Länderbank (Bank Austria)
1010, Stephansplatz 2
Tel: 513 16 26-0

Creditanstalt Bankverein
1010, Schottengasse 6–8
Tel: 531 31

Travel Agencies

Kuoni
1010, Wipplingerstrasse 34
Tel: 535 36 06

Cosmos
1010, Kärntner Ring 15
Tel: 515 33-0

Ibusz
1010, Kärntnerstrasse 26 (specialists for Hungary)
Tel: 512 78 79

Ruefa
1010, Rotenturmstrasse 20
Tel: 534 04

Neckermann Österreich
1070, Mariahilferstrasse 20
Tel: 96 24-0

Rent-a-Car

Avis
1010, Opernring 1
Tel: 587 62 41
Vienna Airport, Tel: 711 10/2700

Budget
1030, Am Stadtpark (Hilton Hotel)
Tel: 75 65 65
Vienna Airport, Tel: 711 10/2711

Hertz
1010, Kärntner Ring 17
Tel: 512 86 77

FURTHER READING

History
Austria, Empire and Republic, by Barbara Jelavich (Cambridge University Press).
Baroque and Rococo, edited by Anthony Blunt (Granada).
Dissolution of the Austro-Hungarian Empire, by J W Mason (Longman.)
The Fall of the House of Habsburg, by Edward Crankshaw (Penguin, 1983).
The Habsburg Monarchy, by A J P Taylor (Penguin, 1990).
Mayerling: the Facts behind the Legend, by Fritz Judtman (Harrap, 1971).
Nightmare in Paradise: Vienna and its Jews, by George E Berkley (California University Press).

Art & Literature
The Age of the Baroque, 1610–1660, by Carl J Friedrich (Greenwood Press, London).
Austrian Life and Literature – Eight Essays, edited by Peter Branscombe (Scottish Academic Press).
The Austrian Mind – An Intellectual and Social History 1848–1938, by William M Johnstone (University of California Press).
Music Guide to Austria & Germany, by Elaine Brody (Dodd, 1975).

General
Austrian Cooking, by Gretel Beer (André Deutsch).
Insight Cityguide: Vienna, Apa Publications, 1990.
Insight Guide: Austria, Apa Publications, 1992.
Journeys, by Jan Morris (Oxford University Press, 1984). Collection includes an essay on Vienna.

Fiction
The Third Man, by Graham Greene (Viking, 1950).

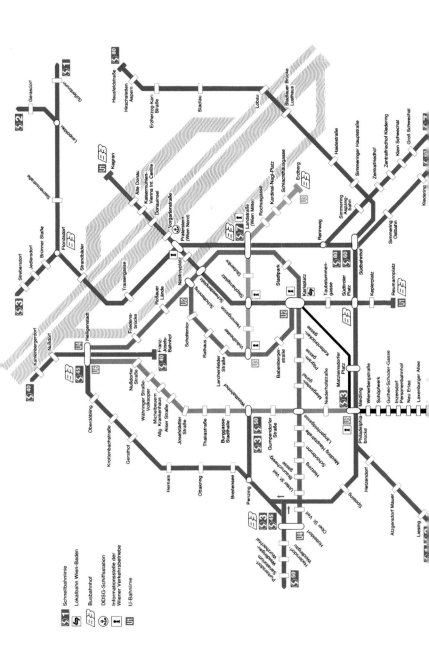

93

ART & PHOTO CREDITS

cover (Houghton Mifflin)	**Robert McLeod**
Photography	**Nicole Schmidt** and
11	**Historisches Museum der Stadt Wien**
20	**J Klinger**
4, 16, 17, 18, 31, 38, 45, 49	**A Laudien**
12, 13, 28, 30, 34, 41, 47, 63, 65, 69, 75	**A Marcheselli**
18, 73, 78, 79, 85, 87	**Viennaslide**
21	**M O Weihs**
10/11, 61	**WFVV**
58	**WFVV-Markowitsch**
48	**WFVV-Mayer**
59	**WFVV-Simoner**
57	**WFVV-Wiesenhof**
36	**G Zugmann**
Illustration, page 50	**Martina Braun**
Designer	**Klaus Geisler**
Cartography	**Berndtson & Berndtson**

INSIGHT GUIDES

COLORSET NUMBERS

You'll find the colorset number on the spine of each Insight Guide.

INSIGHT *Pocket* GUIDES

• •
United States: **Houghton Mifflin Company, Boston MA 02108**
Tel: (800) 2253362 Fax: (800) 4589501

Canada: **Thomas Allen & Son, 390 Steelcase Road East**
Markham, Ontario L3R 1G2
Tel: (416) 4759126 Fax: (416) 4756747

Great Britain: **GeoCenter UK, Hampshire RG22 4BJ**
Tel: (256) 817987 Fax: (256) 817988

Worldwide: **Höfer Communications Singapore 2262**
Tel: (65) 8612755 Fax: (65) 8616438

> **❝** I was first drawn to the Insight Guides by the excellent "Nepal" volume. I can think of no book which so effectively captures the essence of a country. Out of these pages leaped the Nepal I know – the captivating charm of a people and their culture. I've since discovered and enjoyed the entire Insight Guide Series. Each volume deals with a country or city in the same sensitive depth, which is nowhere more evident than in the superb photography. **❞**

Sir Edmund Hillary

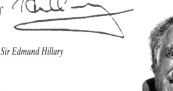